Star Boy 3

Pain...Passion...Forgiveness

"If I had only trusted and believed in your
love I wouldn't be hurting now!"

Tilsa C. Wright

Printed in United States of America
First Printing: December 2012
ISBN – 13: 978-1481250931
ISBN-10: 1481250930

Preface

They say true love will never die; however in this case Brian and Tania are on a journey that only God can predict. If loving Brian is so wrong, she doesn't want to be right.

Will a second chance at love last, as Tania finds herself in a triangle? The only way to find out is to turn the pages of this conclusive series.

Thank Yous

To my ace Keisha Carty, you rock big sister dear. Karlene Gregory my number one fan in Jamaica. Sean 'Father Brooks' Brooks I see you have Star Boy locked in Baltimore MD, Taffari Coke HitSquadd foundation stands tall, Donna-Mae Maitland the Killa's first lady Bless up, Shaunta Swissh I can't wait for your production of... to release, Nicky Blaze, Dj Tc from FlexxFm, Junior Culture, Sharna Jackson, and last but not least all my readers and supporters.

True Friends

My three Kings, Hance Jackson, GranSlam and Kirkland Davis aka Karma-K; you three represent an unbroken mould, the epiphany of true friendship. I don't deserve your support, but no matter what I can count you three. Thanks for being there back in the later part of 2011, a time I will never forget as long as I live.

Kirkland my love for you is profound and will never waver, I will try my very best not to destroy our genuine support for each other. "Our ting solid boss"

GranSlam, while I was behind bars I dialed your number a million and one times, is a wonder you didn't change the number. Thank God for that. While in business meetings you took time out to talk to me, telling me to keep my head up, and to fight them girls off. LOL. Boss you know I had to crack a joke. Bless up my HitSquadd President!

Hance 'sweetheart' Jackson, Camperdown's most famous and loved person, thanks for 20 years of friendship. On the real talk though, I along with girls from school days, Portmore and the Bronx we all see you as a PERFECT GENTLEMAN!

Where is the sunshine after the rain?
What am I going to do with this pain?
Should I medicate? Or should I continue to dedicate half
of my heart?. Hold up correction for I made an exception I
gave you all.

He thinks she loves him, he thinks she can replace me. She
flaunts as though she has replaced me. I was his first; I was
his foundation for true love. (This abstract was written for
my female audience thank you very much).

After finishing the first draft of Star Boy3 I decided to share a youtube video. A very powerful love song that best describes how most women with a broken heart might honestly feel. Google Jon Secada's song Angel, and purchase the album if available.

Baby I tried to forget you, but the light of your eyes still shine, shines like an angel, a spirit that won't let me go.-by Jon Secada.

Ladies my advice to you is, hold on to your Star Boy no matter what! Speaking from experience, my absolute real Star Boy is yet to be replaced. The-Absolute-Best-Fine Wine-And-Dine!

REALITY BOOTH SIX

Roses are red, violets are blue, and sugar is sweet however not as sweet as you Brian Lane! Ha-ha. Very mature right or more like child's play? Star Boy2, what a struggle and a real showdown fight? What can I tell you, many women can relate to Tania on some levels; but let me not talk about you and your relationship; this booth is about me, selfish old me!

So a 60 plus year old Jamaican lady living in Brooklyn bought both part one and two right. Weeks later after reading both copies she decided to interrogate my creative, evasive slick ass.

"Miss Wright, do tell who is Brian Lane?"

"A fictitious person my dear he is not real." I answered with a huge million dollar smile.

"Not a real person my backside, look at your face light up like Christmas tree!" This Star Boy fan wasn't having my BS at all; she wanted me to fess up.

"What can I tell you; we all had or even now have a Star Boy in our life right? However I will keep you posted about the release of part three." And with that I left her hanging, not confirming or denying, this fox was sly, she might be old but certainly she wasn't a Nun from the convent holding confessional beads or a crucifixion at my forehead. My 60 plus year old fan had to dig deeper and come better to get the truth about Mary or in this case Brian Lane...LOL

7

Star Boy 3

Clearly my unnamed Star Boy, who was my first real, true love connection, is to some extent an inspired or one percent responsible for this book series. Well I would like to mess with your thoughts a bit. I will give you a list of names for you to decide who this unnamed Star Boy is. Here begins; Larry, Jack, Tom, Bill and Phil. Your guess is as good as mine. Gotcha!

Let's face it sometimes our High School sweethearts are usually a springboard for years to come; helping to decide what qualities to look for and the works in a relationship. But I know you want me to share more, so here we go. My Mr. Unnamed was sweet, charming, caring, loving, stubborn, and hot headed at times; he was my friend and then some. A guy difficult to figure out most times just had to take him as is, he was guarded, however a buttercup when you do get close to him emotionally that is. He wasn't a monster, just a ladies' man; he kissed plenty but never tells. His touch as you have noticed was unforgettable, his canvas of love bites or hickies was refreshed each week without fail. I tell you those love bites were an indication to other chaps that I was off the market. Well hit him up for your own experience ladies, and believe me you will be hooked, lined and really hooked, and forever wanting more and more and more.... Overkill with descriptions right? Giving him tons of credit... well most of his ex-girl friends pretend, but they know the real deal, that just like KFC, he is finger licking GOOD!

I shared the cake, no correction they got crumbs, my side dishes only got my left over and a shattered glass for memories. There was one side dish in particular, nerd looking thick glasses short pushy little chick, thought she could take my position. Her services was short lived, sent her packing and crying, boo woo. Imagine I travelled for three weeks and this girl was in my cool aide SMH!

Some women only want a man after he is spoken for, when he was available, well not really, Mr. Unnamed always had a bat in hand playing test, or hitting sixes, or like baseball homeruns. They saw his value, however I treasured his worth, not on paper, but for whom he was. Yes the good, the bad and very much so ugly, and the blinding ugly face he has. Anyways many girls thought he was ugly, many, lots! But that didn't matter to me. So obviously I liked him even more for himself and not for some fairytale. The few who got a taste of him were considered season girls, side dish special who lacked taste and flavor, like Shaggy said "This wasn't me".

Oh yeah might I add that his unique juicy lips, massaging fingers and sturdy tools of the trade to name a few of his treasures was part of his valued package; PRICELESS!... Again I'm giving him tons of credit here folks, ha-ha, me and my choice of words yet I failed CXC English twice, wrote four books and counting, well go figure.

Yes I have painted my love for him, or better yet what attracted me to him. I know you must ask so did he loved you, or liked you T? I would answer that with a ninety percent yes and a ten percent of doubt, as you already knows it is very challenging to capture a man's heart completely. In the beginning I was sure; he placed me on a pedestal towards the end of our five years physical union fest, that's when my position became questionable, and overtaken. However during my reign Mr. Unnamed was GREAT to me. He let his guard down, allowed me to enter his life, his world. But his young cheating ways, and he deciding to shut me out after breaching our trust, shutting me out in a manner that appeared to me at the time of being somewhat ungrateful; lead me to later mutilating his heart into irreparable pieces. It never hurts to speak the truth right?

Alright, enough of this true love factor, story lines are running rampant in my head, let me move forward, by thanking my friends, fans, and supporters for this journey.

So go head and relax, pour some Hennessey Star Boy3 is about to take you to rehab!

Angela
Labeled Package

"Why are you arresting me officer she attacked me?"

"You are a known troublemaker, for all I know you started this brawl!"

"Oh really now, Officer Know All! When I press charges against your dumb ass for arresting a pregnant woman who was assaulted by…." I felt a sudden wetness between my legs. "If I lose this baby because of that damsel in distress and her double dipping husband I will make their lives a living hell!"

"Officer Martin please call for an ambulance, this one water just broke. If you ask me today is her lucky day, we tired of seeing your bleach out face at the station."

"Filthy officer Dick, you have a problem with me? Or the fact that I never gave you a percentage from the loot the last time you blackmailed me?" I wanted to muster up some saliva and spit directly in his pimple ugly looking face, but pains were running through my entire body.

Officer Dickson had it in for me since my second arrest. Dickson, Dickey, I called him Dick for short was a popular officer known in the streets for being corrupt, forceful and violent. Oh Lord these pains are coming very rapid I am so not in control to even know the time between contractions. I am plenty things but not a sidewalk delivery baby mother, especially for a local celebrity. Having Brian Lane's baby on the sidewalk wasn't in my cards. So many things weren't in my cards, for starters not knowing if this child is for either Brian or Dudley which was an emotional madness I created. Going into an undermining deception to destroy Tania Watson nine months ago seemed joyful and perfect. Miss Prissy Tania had it all, the luxury comfort and prestige and including Brian, her meal ticket to the Cricket Wives Club. I had known Brian before Tania ever set eyes on him back in High School, at first he was a play toy in bed because we were young. However when he chose Tania back then at school, I was bent on destroying her happy perfect picture life with him. Just the mere thought of her gives me a headache, that self-righteous all up in Brian buttocks, blinding her from seeing she wasn't the only woman in his life. Her beloved Brian sure had her in complete darkness.

"Marsha!" I yelled in agony, where the hell is that middle factor chick. One minute she was here with me, the next standing and comforting Miss Prissy; I told her long time ago she will have to choose someday. Yeah like seriously!

"Angela, hold tight I hear the sirens they must be headed in this direction. Dam everything takes a longtime to come in this country. In the States an ambulance arrives in two minutes. Here is like eternity, this Government spends money on the wrong sectors if you should ask me."

"Marsha shut your ass up about the Jamaican Government, my backside is in pain. You've been living in the States for few years and you coming here to compare and judge. Kiss my teeth; well go back to your precious States!"

"I will ignore your ignorant comment, since you are truly in pain. Just don't take your Brian and Tania Lane frustration out on me! I told you long time ago to leave them two alone, now look at the mess you created, all three of you making scandal."

"You know what Marsha, go comfort Tania; I be cannot bothered with your judgmental comments right now. Since I took Brian alone in my bed, let me have his child alone. Because I know for hell Brian and I never had a threesome with your stuck up ass."

I might be carrying a labeled package, which was made out of adultery; I will have to live with this fact for the rest of my life. However Marsha's stuck up guilty comments; I am just not in the mood for it right now, what I need right now is something for this pain, and this child out, for heaven sakes the baby's head is right there!

Brian
Confused

"Officer please do not arrest my wife, I am begging you." I pleaded; Tania will never forgive me for causing all this…

"Which one is your wife?" Officer Ho-Sang asked with a smirk on his fat round Chinese looking face.

"The one in the Jeep, I really don't care for the other…loud mouth character."

"Really now, she has been yelling non-stop it's your baby she's having on the sidewalk, a celebrity at that." Both officers were having a field day; this scandal is going to make station house jokes for days. I can just picture all the laughter and rumors; truth be told, I will have to face it, face the backlash from sleeping with the enemy. Angela was a drama queen; leave it to her to pretend being my wife, adding more insult to injury.

The other half of my heart, have me in both shock and confusion just didn't think she would fight another woman, much less trail my moves. What must I do at this point? My affair will now be televised I'm certain Patrick will use this to make a killing. The man has a reality TV Show for heaven sake, what was Tania thinking? Yes I caused this pain, the disgrace, I did have ample time to be honest with T. A moment of weakness and loneliness led me between the legs of a disgusting woman; who I knew wasn't the one but her walls were wide open, tempting and satisfying the void I felt being separated from Tania. For a second I totally forgot about Cricket, I cannot afford to lose that along with my family! What a confusion and chaotic mess my life has become! It went from making love to my wife couple hours ago, to being the center of an uptown public scandal. DAMN! This is beyond a mess, it's an earthquake measuring 10.0, shattering the very core of my marriage.

I could sure use Dudley's help right now; wonder what he is up to?

"Hello Swing, what's going on?" Dudley answered his cell after the second ring.

"Can you meet me at Peppers Restaurant right now, it's an emergency?"

Tania
Bars of Soap!

I really need to lose that cheaters name! Tania
Watson, that's my name, starting over, going back, or call it
a rebirth of some sorts; after the embarrassing fight that
landed me in jail for assaulting, and battering a pregnant
woman, and with all that, Angela didn't lose the baby, that
gold digger! I should have put her sleazy sleep around
bleached face in a coma. Trust me she had this beat down a
long time coming, provoking me since school days, she
lucky she I didn't crack her skull.

So what you think, I would be still pining over my
love for Brian Christopher Lane? No way, not whatsoever!
Pine is for women who actually use Pine-Sol to disinfect
the funks from their husband infidelities, and then continue
to be with them over and over, like using an old mop of
Pine-Sol. Surface cleaning, not me! Brian Christopher Lane
is HISTORY!

"Lane Tania! Pack up your belongings, lucky you, your bail
was posted!" Yelled the annoying officer from her post,
which was next to a heavy metal door. That very same
metal door which I was about to exit, was a metaphor
mirroring my life, walking and leaving Brian's cheating
ways; and the disgusting situations in this filthy jail house
behind me for good.

Why has, or do women like myself, become
victims from falling in love with men we deem our Prince,
to having our lives end up like this? Back in school I had

my head on my shoulders, I knew exactly what I wanted, why did I settle. I need more than just a shrink, I need a complete new brain, a brain that would be totally rid of Brian Lane every physical, sexual, darn it his very existence!

"Sister dear…Tania Watson I am over here." I vaguely heard a familiar voice, as my inner thoughts overpowered my senses, and surroundings. I was in deep depressing thoughts I didn't even recognized my baby boy smiling, and stretching his hands for me to hold him. Jackie and little B stood couple feet from the final gate, I was so traumatized I walked like a zombie. Yes I was excited, happy, to see friendly faces, but I was so numb I couldn't even express these feelings. However my life has taken a serious nose dive!

"Tania, Tania." Jackie called out to me twice, bringing me back to consciousness. She wrapped her arms around me as my little man squeeze in the middle of us. I took him from Jackie's arms, kissing him all over his face. What a joy to have him, his short arms were wrapped tightly around my neck.

"I love you little B, I promise never to leave you like this." Releasing his hold from around my neck, now resting his head on my shoulders; I could feel the love, the bond that mothers share with their off spring. It was going to be me and my little B from this point on, just the two of us.

I decided to stay by Jackie for about a week; I needed to really clear my head. Going back to my marital home was not an option. I walked around the house like a zombie, trapped with thoughts of fear and unknown facts about my future, not sure how to fight, or where do I begin to rationalize my life. My world was all about Brian, and our marriage. How do I really picking up the pieces, how do I come from that which I created, a soap-opera media scandal. Out of stupidity and anger I had Patrick film the fight between myself and Angela, which he edited and televised on the local networks, youtube, and published on a few local blog sites. *'Cricketer's infidelity caught red handed, wife beats pregnant mistress.'* This went viral the very next day; the local and international newspapers and other platforms were having a field day. There was no way I could show my face in public. That explained the cameras outside the jail; I was so down and out that I failed to pay attention to the handful of reporters.

Brian called at least three times, I ignored him. He was afraid to come by Jackie's, knowing very well the reporters might trail him, which would add more wood to the fire.

"Sister dear, are you awake?" Jackie asked from outside the bedroom door. "I prepared breakfast, ackee with salt fish fried breadfruit and Milo."

"I am up; give me 30 minutes I will be dressed and ready to enjoy my big sis cooking." Food was the least of my worries; I hardly ate a fork or a spoon of decent meal for days now. The first time Brian and I separated that was heart wrenching, this time it feels like a funeral. Depressed and borderline suicidal, getting out of bed each morning felt like a painful task. I need to shower, or take a bath in a tub, with a bar of soap to wash my painful dirty life, my past, and remove the entire bars of what was left of my marriage. I was a prisoner, trying to wash away the stained ink of infidelity.

Angela
Blood Work

"Push Angela, push this will be over soon!" Doctor Clarke was so calm giving me instructions. My back was paining as if I was a beaten slave, my vagina felt like thick skin being ripped apart; never again will I go through this, neither Brian nor Dudley is worth this.

After three plus hours a tiny 6lbs baby crying girl was born. I looked at her as I held her in my arms for the first time, I was happy but yet sad. Not sure who was her Daddy, I hoped it was Brian for obvious reasons, pin this child on him would give me a long term reason to be a factor in his life. My hopeful baby daddy wasn't answering my calls; guess he went to the police station to comfort his precious Tania.

"Dudley, I need you right now and if Brian is with you bring him along. For whatever reason Brian is not answering my calls it would be nice for him to meet his newborn."

"How is the baby?" He asked what a good friend he was, Dudley's agenda is so twisted and I fell right into it perfectly. I pray this scheme of ours doesn't blow up.

"She is fine Dudley, how soon before you get here?"

"Give me at least an hour, or so. As you can imagine Brian is an emotional wreck right now, so if he doesn't respond in the manner you would like, just hold tight, and give him time to eventually come around."

As promised both men showed up at my bedside within the hour. The devil stood on the right of my bed, while the man I've always wanted stood at my left. I got into character immediately as they both walked in my hospital room.

"See what your wife did to my face? I am scared for life thanks to her; however looking on the bright side I had a girl, we have a baby girl Brian." I knew what buttons to press; Tania made playing the victim very easy, and one thing I know how to do is manipulate a man into getting what I want.

"Drama Queen, always trying to pin the blame on someone besides yourself; Tania is not your problem you are your own worst enemy." Brian answered with disgust and regret.

"Must I hear this again, you attacking me again, and again? Brian do me a favor, sign the baby's birth papers and wait for my lawyer's phone call about child support. I will show you a real drama queen."

"Ok you two no need to escalate this situation even further. Swing I know how you feel right now, and Tania, oops sorry Angela just relax, you called us so we are here to comfort you. We are going to step outside so Brian could cool off, I will make sure he signs the papers and take you home safely if the hospital is ready for you to go home today." Dudley the man of reasoning, the devil always has a plan up his sleeves, trust and believe he never fails to deliver bad deeds.

After Dudley and Brian left my room, I began feeling pain on my left side, very sharp and unbearable. "Nurse, nurse, I am in pain." I yelled forgetting that there is a call button; my loud mouth will do the trick, after all a celebrity was in the building and I just gave birth to his child.

Two nurses came in my room, one spoke and the other listened. I sensed something else was going on outside my room, they were doing lots of eye contact between them, as the senior nurse gave me something for the pain, which by the way subsided in 5 minutes.

"Nurse Carla is there a problem?" it was very noticeable and made me very uncomfortable.

"The gentleman, sorry Mr. Lane insists on having a paternity test done before he signs the papers. We cannot proceed with the test without your consent."

I cannot have him do this now, especially with Dudley being here. Oh Lord Father how do I get out of this madness! Yes I slept with Dudley the same times I did with Brian, however I plotted with Dudley and he never asked if it was his. Guess he never cared, he reminds me of a dog in heat, they chase you day and night, as soon as the female dog is pregnant it's on to the next. It was embarrassing to say the very least, and I could see they were having pity on me. Here I am bragging about a celebrity being the father of my new born, and he is here demanding the legitimacy of my claim.

"Thanks nurse Carla; I will be handling the situation from here on." I was becoming sleepy; my body was very tired from the ordeal of giving birth, and now this. For whatever reason the phone in my room rang, nurse Carla answered, she looked at the other nurse, and then asked if I was ok then rushed out the room. Not sure what the emergency was, well must had been job related.

Couple of hours well must have passed; I slept like a baby out for the count. I woke up to a bouquet of red roses on my side table, there was a note. As I reached for it the door opened, it was Nurse Carla.

"Oh let me get that for you Angela." She offered so sincerely.

"Thanks, I truly appreciate your kindness for the past two days. I came here on hells stretcher, and you are making me feel a great sense of comfort."

I opened the note, it was from Dudley it read; *'to protect the validity of our plans I must not see, or talk to you anymore. I have to be supportive of Brian's frame of mind.'*

So now I have to fend for myself, first I get knocked up by either him or Brian, then during the pregnancy Brian completely ignores me, Tania Watson fights me in public, as a result I almost got arrested, this fight was all over the television as a breaking Entertainment Report on our local networks. To top everything off, Brian insisting on a paternity test, now the snake Dudley is bailing on me! I feel as though I should die, right here, right now, which would be perfect given the fact I am already at the hospital.

Nurse Carla saw the look on my face, and could tell something was wrong. However she too seemed to have been going through a rough day.

"Angela, I am afraid there is some complication with your baby's breathing…"

"What? When did this started nurse? Why I wasn't notified immediately?"

"Her condition changed while you were asleep, didn't think it would be right to wake you seeing that you were experiencing pain."

"What happened to my baby nurse Carla? She only got here few hours now, what could possibly be wrong?" Oh Father in heaven, please forgive me of all my wrong doings, please do not, oh I beg and plead do not take my child away from me. Oh have mercy for I know I have sinned in thy sight.

Carla left, she did her job to deliver the news and just left, I am here alone in both physical and emotional pain. A bad person feels pain too, I know we come across being heartless but pain is all we know, all I have ever known.

"Nurse Carla, Doctor Clarke!" I yelled repeatedly, I was frantic and demanded some answers, what's wrong with my baby God damn it!

"Ms. Ricketts, my name is Nurse Wills I am Nurse Carla's supervisor, what seems to be the problem?"

"The problem is your worker Nurse Carla is incompetent, how dear her come in here tell me that there is something wrong with my child and then just walk away. I need some answers and for somebody please take me to see my baby."

"Ok I will handle this situation from here on. In the meantime relax, calm down Ms. Ricketts your blood pressure is high so you really need to calm down." Nurse Wills was older than Nurse Carla; she has a better sense of dealing with me. Bottom line she took control and had empathy. Nurse Carla acted like a coward, then why work in the field if you cannot handle patients like me.

My poor baby girl, I met you couple hours now, not being able to see you, nor even give you a name, and now for you to go through complications with me at your bedside. Oh God I need to hold her.

Tania
Rock Bottom

Lights, camera, action! This was no more, my life had become a shoe box I had allow myself to fall in self pity; I had no strength I was boxed in a mindset, a complete entrapment to give up on life. Why me? Why such a trial and tribulation? I've loved this man with all my entire being, and yet he does the most unforgiving thing ever, it's like the title of the movie 'Sleeping with the Enemy'. I am not even asking how to bounce back, just take this pain away, even it means ending my life, I already feel dead, what the use of me still breathing.

"Tania, open the door!" My dearest mother and Jackie who had keys to my apartment but not to my bedroom were demanding to come in. I usually take sleeping pills each night; but since I am now pregnant I didn't want to compromise my baby's condition. Although it was much easier that way to fall asleep, oh God it has been so difficult to really sleep these past weeks. If not the pills then it would be something strong, like Vodka, suppressants were clearly a perfect way out for me right now. Given my borderline suicidal frame of mind, it would be best if I left both alone.

"Ok give me a second!" I wasn't in the mood for company, much less an intervention from these two, I know it's out of love. Love there goes that word, the word and emotions that have me in the pits.

"What do you two want from my life? Can a sister be alone in her own space, please?"

"Fresh mouth, with your fat pregnant ass, look at you come on get it together! Shake this slump off and revive yourself, for God's sake you are expecting a baby stop being selfish." Leave it to mother to keep it real, and really bagger my ass with harsh words. Jackie her disciple stood shaking her head, mother had to have the only and last say we both knew it.

"Ok I am revived; you have my full attention now." I was sure they would buy my con.

"Who you kidding chile, you need professional help because this time I want him out of your head for good!" Mother's tone mean business, she wasn't joking.

"Jackie how is little B?" I had to deflect or this woman was going to drive me insane.

"He is good, staying by his father for couple days." Not the life I wanted for him, bouncing from house to house like a cricket ball, just picture him rolling from slip to boundary. God knows he is spoiled, but I just don't care for him becoming confused being around different house hold.

"Did you tell Brian I want a divorce, not next never but actually now?"

"Yes, and he is not entertaining the idea. Brian would prefer to work things out Tania."

"Guess he is more twisted than I thought." Mother had to add her two senses.

"Besides all that, Angela baby died 24 hours after giving birth."

"Jackie why are you telling me this; I don't care about her?"

"Tania, you have locked yourself in depression going on three months, you need to face the reality of what has happened. Angela can press charges against you for the death of her baby, just hear me out for a second. So please brace yourself for what's going on in the real world."

The real world, what's that? Press charges, against whom? No need to work myself up with Angela's issue, I have to focus on getting my life back. My frame of mind is so fragile one minute I want to give up, and then the next rebound. As for Angela and the assault charges the Judge threw it out, don't ask me on what grounds. I just figure he was one of Brian's inner circles, you know how it is when you are associated with people of power and influence, you can bloody near get away with murder.

So after mother and Jackie left my apartment, I began going through paper work. I had to separate what I truly owned, or acquired with my money, from what was given to me by Brian. One thing about Brian, he knows how to save, and giving up half would be a real court house fight. I need to prepare myself for this battle; it will not be easy for sure. Jackie knows an excellent divorce attorney, James McCorkley, his last name sounds weird. Word around town is, McCorkley was the cleaners, and his rates are not cheap. Well Brian should have thought of how much it would cost him if he cheated, Mr. Cleaners and I will be having a field day.

I feel like the road ahead will be very rocky, but I am determined to face the music with Brian and his attorney. Now that I have mustered up the courage, let me pour myself a glass of wine, wait I am pregnant. How could I forget another baggage from this failed marriage, a glass of fruit juice will do. Guess I need to stop doing a number of things including loving this knuckle head Brian Lane. Oh Lord Father give me a life worth living, one filled with happiness and surely less complications.

Being 3 months pregnant, is actually 3 months since the fight, a very televised fight as though it were a Saturday night and the world was glued to their pay-per view channel to see a Mike Tyson big ticket fight. For this reason I stayed hidden away at home, thanking God for waking me up this morning although I am in pain and feeling nauseous I must get out and not miss my appointment with James. What should I wear? Need to attire as though my spirits are up, but on the other hand I scream victim, and deserving half of every dime Brian Lane posses.

The only thing I could squeeze my fat buns in was a jeans skirt I have from being pregnant with little B. Good thing I didn't give away all my maternity clothes, not sure why because Brian and I were separated and the thought of having more children was farfetched.

"Good morning Mrs. Lane, Mr. McCorkley will be with you shortly please make yourself comfortable and have a seat …" The receptionist pointed to a three piece expensive leather sofa. James office was on the 14th floor overlooking Kingston Jamaica busy streets, not forgetting to mention the fumes from several factories located closer to the wharf.

To occupy my time while waiting to see James, I flipped through the pages of Essence, Vogue and a few others I wasn't familiar with. He should have one that caters to pregnant divorce women, which will be a hot seller giving how unfaithful men can be, period! I know I am not making sense here but go figure; my emotions are like at a playground.

Sitting here is like meditating at a cross roads, I am hearing two other voices of reason. One says give Brian another chance and the other says take him to the cleaners James will help you get all what you deserve. Picture the devil in a blue dress, and the angel in white, who do I really listen to? Oh Lord! Do you see what I mean, how on earth can I picture these two wearing dresses, when they are suppose to be male figure.

"Come on in Miss Watson, sorry for keeping you waiting so long." James was handsome and if he wasn't already taken, I am sure most of his female clients would be more than happy to throw him a Kit-Kat at least once or twice each week.

But who is that? Is that who I think it is? Miss Jamaica! Talk about high profile clientele. Wow, I remember reading about her failed relationship with that well-known music producer from Portmore. I guess she decided to really clean his bank account. She was in James's office, guess her appointment was before mine.

"That's fine James I know how it goes. I actually enjoyed browsing through several magazines."

"Glad you did. Please do have a seat, and so tell me how are you really doing Miss Watson?" James asked as he pointed in the direction of a chair facing his.

"These past couple of days much better, in comparison to couple months ago, it felt as though my days were numbered, each second the clock ticked I wasn't sure if that would be my last."

"Would you like for me to arrange counseling? This will help with your litigation proceedings, paints a vivid picture that you are indeed the victim, and makes the negotiations much easier and clearly in your favor."

"Seeing a shrink, I am not comfortable with the idea reason being I am pregnant and Brian's lawyer might use it as a tool to gain full custody. James I am not prepared to lose my children to him." I immediately started to cry, this entire process wasn't going to be easy at all.

"Do you need time to rethink the divorce proceedings? If no, then I must prepare your defense, and from where I am sitting Miss Watson it's a 50/50. Normally I prefer, or should I say my track record is putting women in your situation in the drivers' seat at let's say 85/15 negotiating control."

"Why 50/50?" I was in shock at this number.

"Well Brian has a strong case against you, citing you are responsible for the public humiliation and media scandal. Then there are also rumors of you getting a kickback from Patrick's video production, and if found true will pose trouble for your case."

"Oh my goodness, that's not even true!" Calm down Tania, I said quietly to myself, no need to work up any more stress. I've been so depress that almost all the time I forget about my pregnancy.

"James may I have a glass of water?" He got out his plush black leather chair; I couldn't help noticing his tight built body frame. James was sexy, an eye candy a real chocolate. What am I doing? This man is my attorney, I am suppose to be depressed, the victim, not the slut like Angela.

30

"To add more salt to Brian's wounds, or in this case financial outlook, not only does he have this legal proceeding with you, but he has been pleading his case to The Board of Directors. They suspended him from the team; being very new to the squad, and the players association is having a difficult time defending him."

"James, I see we are in for a battle, a very long one at that."

"The board will decide Brian's fate in two weeks, and from what I am hearing from very good sources, it's not looking good for him. The outcome will most likely affect his earnings, which will leave you only entitled to whatever he has now."

"Brian is worth close to 10million before the drama, he was expected to at least increase it to about 100million over the next 2 years given his Star Boy status." I added a few known facts his business manager had pointed out when he bought the house few months back. He was set to earn a killing in endorsements.

"True, my team did their research and come up with figures close to your estimation. However 10million in this economy is not much to live on with two children plus alimony."

"Wow, I didn't realize the details of this proceeding I honestly thought it would be a done deal, the judge would just evaluate his assets and award me half."

"Miss Watson, on the very low end of the spectrum the courts may award you $150,000 per month for child support plus alimony. This figure is peanuts; I recommend we aim for a minimum of $325,000."

Star Boy 3

I know Brian very well, these figures will send him through the roof, but there I go thinking about his feelings and not what I deserve for tolerating his cheating ways. James went over so many details about my case; I had an instant headache. Our life, correction my life with Brian since 17 will be on trial before a judge who will determine how we should emotionally and financially separate for good.

Remembering this hit song written by Bryan Adams, these words best describes the meaning of loving someone. How do I move on to share a pure innocent love connection again? Only God has the answer.

Still feels like the first night together
Feels like the first kiss
It's getting better baby. No one can better this
Still holding on. You're still the one
First time our eyes met. Same feeling I get
Only feels much stronger
I wanna love you longer
Please forgive, I know not what I do
Please forgive me I can't stop loving you-Bryan Adams check his video on youtube.

Angela
Stop the Hate

How do I stop the pain from ripping my heart out?
Back in high school I had an abortion, well actually 2,
however it is a different feeling when you give birth and
your baby dies. For some reason her heart stopped, now
months later the guilt of being involved with Brian for the
wrong reasons weighs heavy on my conscience.

"You have reached the voicemail of Dudley, leave me a
message or a text." That's all I have been getting when I
call this bastard's number, just like that he dropped me
from his disturbed plot to ruin Tania's life. It didn't matter
what time of the day I called Dudley he refuses to answer. I
wonder who will be his next conspirator, to work with his
revengeful ass. There must be something constructive for
me to do, I cannot continue to sulk in sorry. Relaxing is a
thing of the past, wait who is at my door so early in the
morning?

"Who is it?"

"Brian, let me in we need to talk."

To what do I owe this visit I thought quickly, we
haven't spoken in two months. Our last exchange was that
day he and Dudley showed up at the hospital after I gave
birth.

"Good morning Brian, why are you here?"

"Am I disrupting your man hunt session, we all know you bounce back fast despite any drama that arises in your life." "What a mean and awful thing to say, can't say something nice about a person then hush… I am sure you must have learned this growing up in your world of association Brian Cheating Lane!"

"Get over yourself Angela, your reputation speaks more volume than that long winded sentence, or speech. Save it for someone who cares to be impressed by you."

"Which brings me back to the question as to why are you here Brian?"

"Dudley tells me you have been blowing his phone up, obviously he refuses to be involved in your dimensional or delusional mental fragment of being with me."

"Being with me wasn't a problem back in High School right? When you and your precious Tania separated, whose legs did you run into and came in, Brian?"

"That's the problem with women like you, you all give easy access and expect us to commit and fall in love instantly. You are sick to think I would honestly take you serious over Tania. Calling you a rebound wouldn't be appropriate, at this point you are worst than a joke."

"Our baby died Brian, and these are the filthy things you are going to say to my face?" I felt tears running down my cheeks. God why are you doing this to me?

"What do you mean by our baby? I never acknowledge that child! For all I know it's not mine. Stop using the baby crutch Angela I am tired of it. Besides she is dead, get a grip and move on, and seriously stay out of my life."

34

I slapped Brian in his face, and made sure my fingers sting and scratched his handsome face.

"How dare you talk to me like that? Who the hell you think you are?

He had the nerve to push me, causing me to fall landing on the carpet in the living room. He then wrapped his arms around my neck damn near choking me.

"Let go of me Brian!" I fought back, I wanted to knock his lights out, how dear him?

"You are nothing but a nasty whore Angela, nothing but an easy F...k!"

"How dear you Brian Lane! Leave now before I call the police! Get out; I never want to be your pity fuck at least not anymore, especially now that you have lost everything. All that you earned is down the drain, and oh boy am I happy to see you flat on your face. You are a bastard, and I am a lot of things according to you and the rest of the world, but Tania did you right by video recording what took place at Peppers. Having it all over the media cost you both her and your precious, prestigious career. Get out! Get out Brian! Pay back is a bitch and you are getting yours!"

He was shocked, but who cares I had to defend myself. When someone attacks you what do they expect? Brain left my apartment, upset and speechless, I sure hit him where is hurts the most. He lost Tania, and to add more salt to his cheating wounds The Cricket Board suspended him for breach of moral clause outlined in his contract. He might be out for at least 3-5 years, as for

Tania, she hired the best Attorney who held a huge press conference outlining the details of her divorce demands. Brian Christopher Cheating Lane was doubled screwed, and that served him right!

Tania
Exposed Conference

"Hello Tania speaking." I answered my cell politely not sure whose number was calling at 8AM on a Saturday at that.

"How are you doing Tania, it's me Marsha?" The referee has finally decided to reach out after all this time, I wonder to what I owed this pleasure, you never know what's up her sleeves.

"I am doing good, only have 3 more months before popping this baby out. Where are you calling from?" I had to ask since she is now married to a Cricketer and her travelling schedule is very unpredictable.

"Jamaica flew in last night from Australia. I am here for a week and would like to visit you and the..."

"That's not such a good idea Marsha, after what happened the last time, it's hard for me to be around you knowing you knew Angela was pregnant with Brian's baby, seeing you will only be stressful and I don't need that for my baby or my health right now."

"Fair enough, I totally understand how you feel; however I do hope you can move pass this someday soon as I would love for us to reestablish our friendship Tania."

"Well we will see about that, I have your numbers and perhaps one of these days I will reach out. Take care and I wish nothing but happiness for you and hubby."

I had to hang up, dealing with Marsha or even seeing her is just something not worth doing right now it was bad enough I had to see Brian every weekend, who was a painful reminder of Angela. Speaking of the devil he should be here around 10AM to pick up little B; let me drag my fat buttocks and get him ready for his Dada. I swear this child is 2 going on 22, time sure is flying just now he will be having company, and I can just picture these two pumpkins driving me nuts for sure.

"Brian junior where are you." I called from the hall way, he is very independent these days, he gets up walks to the living room turns the television on and quietly watches cartoons. That's my boy, smart, independent, and fresh with his words, anyhow he is the center of my world for now until baby number two comes, 3 more months and counting.

"Tania I am running late, I should be there around 12:30." Brian on the other end of the house phone, I wonder who or what has him late. Then again that's not my problem to focus on, as long as I don't deny him visitation during our divorce proceedings, which by the way is taking longer than I expected. Yeah not putting up a fight, or denying visits or time with his son strengthens my case for sole; denying will only make matters worse.

Documenting his tardiness only makes him look irresponsible.

"Ok see you around then."

Little B for sure fell asleep, and I was becoming restless waiting for Brian who is very late, it's now 2PM and no sight or sound from him; and trust I won't call him. Boy was I hungry every hour on the hour, pregnancy take a great toll on your body and not to mention your appetite. The doctor said my weight gain was ok, not in excess, however I disagree with him, I feel like a huge house and this child was roaming all about. I swear he doesn't know how to stay still.

So Brian decided to show up close to 3PM; how convenient for him it's a good thing I didn't have plans or else he and I would be have war of words.

"Sorry for being extremely late T, this won't happen again."

"Brian, you are always sorry, everything about you these days are plain out right pathetic."

"Tania I deserve that, but relax yourself and get over yourself as well. I am not here to argue, I've apologized now move on."

"Move on! For heaven sake practice those words and do just that for me please MOVE ON! Stop prolonging this divorce proceeding, let me move on with someone else a real responsible man at that."

He became quiet, completely shut down, Brian was not accustom to me speaking so blunt not to mention me saying I want to move on with someone else. That bruised his manly ego; practically cutting him deep like a chef's 7 inch blade. Brian left with little B he didn't outer another word, and I did the same.

Well finally some peace and quiet, having the house to myself was priceless, no Little B running around like batman or superman. Then adding the sometimes discomforting pregnancy factor makes it even better for me to relax and enjoy my own lonesome company for now. However after this child is born it will be noisy town. Oh no here goes the ringing telephone, guess I spoke too soon and like clockwork my sister and mother called me 3-way. Leave it to my annoying two-o to disrupt me quiet flow.

"Tania what are you doing fat prego woman?" Jackie asked jokingly.

"What pregnant women do, sleep, eat, and pass gas."

"Stop being silly sister dearest. Listen up mother and me are coming to get you in the morning."

"What is the occasion? This sound too good to be true, you two are always busy on a Sunday therefore spill your gust Jackie."

"Hush your mouth Tania, just pack an overnight bag, we have a surprise that you need or damn near deserve." Mother hen finally spoke, of course she was being demanding or lack of a better word commanding.

What can I do when Jackie and my mother gang up on me makes no sense saying no, there's no use fighting or arguing I won't win for a plate of ackee and codfish; besides I am a sucker for surprises.

"All right, all right I give up no resistance here. What time you two bounty hunters coming to get me?"

"9AM, prepare to be intrigued and have lots of fun." Jackie adding here mystery two senses, she sounded like a little child, yes that was mother's disciple.

"Love you two, see you in the morning, and now get off my phone."

Sleep wasn't in my system anymore; anxiety captured my thoughts, really asking myself what are those two up to? Well many hours later, it's now 8PM and I am feeling a bit hungry I prepared oatmeal and wheat toast, I am just not feeling for heavy food of late my taste buds have been craving for cereals going on 3 weeks now. During my pregnancy with little B I craved plenty fruits, now this one loves cereal, 3 more months, 3 more months of this. Repeat after me, 3 more months, 3 more months, shoot wish it was tomorrow, wow such agony.

Angela
Burning Confession

It's a beautiful weekend ahead, perfect to go shopping, clubbing and even indulge in an intense spa treatment. Time for me to bounce back to normalcy, at least try to. Not having a man in my web right this minute feels good, this is a first for me, and it only makes sense since I need to heal both my body and mind. After seeking counseling, I have come to realization that my life has been a train wreck, all because I wanted Brian to fulfill a void that was lacking from my family circle.

Outside of Brian I have had many men, for in my mind it was a controlling mechanizes they gave me money and material things; but love, affection and value weren't on the table. I gave them the juicy prize way too easy, and they enjoyed every bit of it. On the table was my back and they on top pounding away at my physical jewel, similar to a ring that is probably out of shape and size. But who cares, I for certain don't, a real man will love my ring once I am right in the head and demand my emotional worth. Not sure why I am putting myself down like this, I mean when I was younger men complimented my performance, and this made me feel as though I was on top of the world! I told myself my body was in control and my ring wrapped them real tight.

Wait a second Marsha is here for a week, which is great, guess she wants to hang out according to her voice message on my cell. In order to heal, one must forgive and rid the mind of combustions, as per my counselor. Who I like a bit, or have a minor crush on, he is of the Rastafarian belief. To be with him would mean I would have to change my physical appearance and leave all my material things behind. Enough of this counselor crush factor, and let me return Marsha's call.

"Really Marsha, that's what Tania said to you? Oh wow! Can't really blame her, you pose as a constant reminder of what happen in this triangle affair."

"Oh very mature of you Angela, in the past you would be stomping all over her relishing and laughing at her pain. Why the sudden change of heart?"

"In life on must look back and take responsibility for their actions and move along with reality and not fantasy."

"What have you done with Angela Ricketts? Oh bananas I am absolutely loving the new YOU!"

"I have been going to counseling Marsha, after losing the baby the way I did; I wasn't going to make it eat me alive, guess I reached my breaking point."

"I am impressed and certainly proud of you Angie. This is a change in your life I prayed for, God sure does answer prayers."

"Besides I made myself Brian's doormat for a very long time now. Then to add more wood to my demented, fantasy I teamed up with Dudley..."

"What did you say about Dudley? How did you team up with him?" Marsha was sharp and nosy I haven't told a single soul about our deceptive, malicious plans to destroy Tania's fairytale life with her precious Brian Lane.

"Oh you know the usual, said he would convince Brian to be with me during the time he and Tania were separated, but as you can see it backfired and blew up in my face."

"Angela, I am not buying that BS, spill your gust I've known you since high school and can tell when you feeding me crap!"

"Marsha, believe and trust my words, that's all there is to it."

"Alright so be it I will give you the benefit of the doubt, however if you are lying to me Angela, I promise and I am not joking around, I will deliver you to the lion's den and I am dead serious!"

"So this delivery, would be to save your friendship with Tania, and yourself from being in the middle, or out of love for me? Because from where I am sitting Marsha you seem extremely desperate to be in Tania's good grace again."

"Angela save the mellow drama for someone who really cares, if you deal the cards, then confess your filthy hands and stop dancing around the truth, you said earlier you have seek counseling now put it to good use."

"Let's order Marsha before I lose my appetite, everything looks delicious on this menu, what are you having?" I had to end this battle of words before it escalated to something more, Marsha is my friend but sometimes she just get under my skin like a fungus, or a rash which ever she still irritates the life out of me regardless.

"Hmm, speak of the devil in blue dress, here comes Tania, Jackie and their mother. They just got out the car, bet you $1000 they will exit the restaurant once they spot us?"

"So who cares Marsha, we all live in Kingston, it's only natural we have to run into each other at some point. This is not Tania's world, we cannot disappear because we don't get along, and whatever they do it's fine with me. I know for certain I will not leave for the likes of her and her family. Waiter we are ready to order."

Just as Marsha stated, Tania, Jackie and their mother exited as soon as they saw Marsha and I in the restaurant, they sat for about 15 minutes scanned the room and then left. One thing for sure, life isn't fair, Tania is pregnant and here it is I lost my baby, with the likely hood of Brian being the father. You should have seen her wobbling like a duck, while I am still suffering from the loss of my newborn. Again she is giving Brian something I couldn't, a second seed another reason for him to love her even more.

Tania
Dear Diary

Dear diary it's me Tania Watson-Lane, as of today I am still married to the love of my life and miserably pregnant with our second child. Let me recap today's event, mother dearest and Jackie planned a girl's hang out weekend. Two unexpected things happened, one seeing Angela at the restaurant with my former friend Marsha, and second my sister decided to hook me up on a blind date. How sick was that? Just picture me 6 months pregnant on a blind date, it made me look desperate as though I am looking a father for my unborn child. Ricardo Pinnock, he was handsome, charming, but at the end he wasn't my 'B Rock'. Although I'm hurting I still and will forever love him. Which brings me to this poem I wrote, in memory and as a reality, but it doesn't matter how it reads I am feeling stronger each day and eventually I will get over him.

There are days when my thoughts are free,
I block out the memories.
Then there are days I cannot stop the tears,
as there will never be another like you...

I have to go now, feeling a slight discomfort perhaps falling asleep on the pillow that I once shared with Brian ; and looking back at the sweet memories will help calm my nerves and bring

46

some level of comfort. That will be all for now until my next entry.

Marsha
Searching for the Truth

Well I will be in Jamaica for another two more days, and my 10th sense is telling me something is fishy with Angela and Dudley. She accidently trip and was about to spill, but she was quick and I am determined to bring all the worms out. I have heard a bit of rumors here and there about Dudley, saw him at a few events wasn't impressed by his arrogance. Courtney and I have invited him to dinner, at Tracks located somewhere off Constant Spring Road tonight. I plan to lay the foundation to reveal what went down between he and Angela, if it kills me the truth will come out.

"Good evening Courts, man I'm sorry for running so late. Oh Marsha lovely seeing you again, and thanks for the invite."

"You are welcome, and the pleasure is ours." I answered very politely.

"So what's the occasion? What have you and Courtney been up to these past couple months Marsha?" Asked Dudley, the sweet boy at the table, he was so suave and smooth.

"The normal things an engaged couple would be doing, planning a wedding and other future plans." He was taking control of this conversation by

47

asking questions. It's time for me to steer him in my direction, after all it was my interrogation party not his. Dudley was asking or borderline getting into our personal matters. Personally I don't know him like that to even share an ounce of information about our plans. Courtney asked if he could be in the groom's party, I told him after tonight I will give the final say.

"So this is a new restaurant, I've heard a great deal of buzz about it for weeks now. Lovely setting, staff, and music hope the food is just as good. Have you been here before Dudley?"

"Sure Marsha, at least once or twice each week, trust me everything is great here." He replied with a smirk on his face, as if there was more.

"Babes, Dudley is just being himself a typical lady's man. He girlfriend is the Assistant Manager and you scheduling dinner here is an extra perk for him." Courtney explained, patting my leg under the table; after seeing my facial expression. This ugly fool really thought he was God's gift to women; guess all the mirrors are broken at his home.

"So Dudley is she the one? From the look on your face she must be doing something right." I asked, as if he was in custody for some alleged sex crime.

"Marsha it's too soon to jump the broom like you and my dear friend here. Our feelings are still fresh, and young, besides I am not sure if she wants me or my status. When you are a celebrity it's hard to find a true woman." Dudley made perfect sense, just hope he wasn't drawing any references to

Courtney and I, or he will leaving this dinner
regretting ever meeting me.

"Rest assured, Courtney has nothing to worry
about I am his rock as much as he is mine. We have
built a foundation, not flirtation. Feelings and
sensations are for teens, heart and soul more define
our connection; right baby?" I looked into
Courtney eyes, after giving Dudley my speech.

"Absolutely, my love bunny, we have a pure
organic love connection." Courtney was kissing me
gently, validating what his wife to be said.

"You two need a room or something, let's order
some real drinks Courts I am off from training the
next couple of days, so I can consume as much
long island ice tea possible."

"Hold up one minute there, before we all get
wasted Dudley. I would like to meet up with you
one to one tomorrow afternoon, can you pencil me
in.?"

"Certainly, anything for the Captain's wife and as
long as you are not trying to get dirt on my good
friend here, let's meet at Rocks Café around 1PM."

"Don't be silly, I know all that there is to know
about Courtney Washington. We don't have
secrets." I was lying through my teeth, Courtney
was blind to the real reason I wanted to meet
Dudley.

"NO Man Dudley! Marsha has a business deal or prospectus, and being how much you love to invest in Real Estate and other financial securities. This deal I will say is bullet proof from what I've read. I strongly recommend you buy a portion of the shares."

"Courts say no more, your beautiful lady has my attention, can't wait to learn more tomorrow."

We left the restaurant liking each other's company; I was a bit tipsy and feeling to handle my baby seeing I will be with him for only two more nights. On the field and in the media people called him Mr. Courtney Washington, in the bedroom he's my Mr. Body Pierce. His degree of love making was off the charts, at one stage he would be very gentle, romantic, and the next hardcore penetrating me like a needle to a virgin ear.

"You look so edible, plump, and ready to rumble Marsh." One thing about Courtney he gets to the point.

"I sure am, but let me wash up, after all a man must only eat freshly cleaned fruits." After jumping in the shower for a quickie, Courtney laid butt naked on the bed with his tool standing at attention.

Let me give you a brief description, thick long hard, and always ready. I am not sure if it's those peanut punches and other homemade natural drink that makes him have stamina and long home drive. However it didn't matter, Courtney had my parts opened, wet and fit like a perfect ring on a finger, tight and not lose and slippery. He says to me every so often, Marsh you've got the perfect fit baby girl.

Needless to say Courtney and I had more than a ball, last night was porn night which have me now unable to get out of bed and prepare to meet with Dudley. Guess I need two-four Advil for this back pain. Courtney left and would be on the road for the rest of the day. Oh boy do I miss Tania's company, or at the very least being able to talk on the phone. With all the drama between her and Angela over the years, we managed to maintain our friendship, but I guess the last showdown was the straw that broke the Camel's back, figuratively speaking.

It was 85 degrees and I welcomed it wearing a tight fitted blue jeans with a pail orange button front shirt showing a little cleavage, gold accessory, make up well done and to top it off, my hair in a ponytail. I had to get sexy for this creature, who thinks he's God gift to women. Since you can loosen a man's tongue with a little sex appeal, why not use it to my advantage in this case. Dudley was a sucker for some play, and I was willing to go there, well not all the way. However far enough to get the truth out of his spineless ass!

"Are you sure we are meeting for business Marsha? You are looking more ravishing comparing to last night." The first statement to come from predictable Dudley's mouth before I could sit down and make myself comfortable. He apparently arrived 10 minutes before I got here, seeming eager to get something going.

"Must I consider that comment a compliment or an invitation of some sorts?"
"Well there's no shame in mixing a little business with humor, now is there? After all you are spoken for."

"Let's just keep it business here on out. What type of projects have you invested in over the years?" I got straight to the point.

"Mostly start up ventures, like for instance restaurants and entertainment for example concerts and a few popular stage shows. The returns have been remarkable and worth my time; what do you have in mind?"

"Dudley I take it you are familiar with American Idol a popular television program in the United States?"

"Yes, I actually enjoy Simon, though harsh he does make practical sense up and coming artiste needs to hear the truth and not sugar coated comment. In my book constructive criticism it always good, it's just reality."

"In a nutshell I would like to produce and similar platform here in Jamaica, giving talents an opportunity to compete for a record deal with the likes of Tuff Gong."

"Sounds interesting, with so many youths trying to get that big break, this would really be a must see on a weekly basis. Not to also mention being able to identify us with an US brand like American Idol appeals to Jamaicans on a hold. We have lost sight of our culture and fail to be original, however idolize what the Americans do at the drop of a hat." He carefully pointed out. Dudley was not at all that shallow, he does have a business brains it would seem.

I was impressed with Dudley's insight and could tell from the sound of things, getting 5 million from him for starters would be easy like Sunday morning. After presenting proposal documents with solid research figures, I had him sign a confidential agreement along with a commitment letter for a grand total of 30 million dollars. This was small in comparison to some of the other investors with deeper pockets, who basically investing ten times this amount.
One thing was obvious during our meeting, Dudley kept on ignoring a call whosoever they were he was becoming very annoyed and silent his ringer.

"Why are you avoiding her?"

"What makes you think it's a female?"

"Only a woman rings a phone back to back like that, and the fact is men normally answer another man's call."

"True, and true, but this lady is not getting the picture. Been months, and yet she rings like there is 3 alarm fires in her bedroom, which I don't care to put out. Too many firemen have done that, besides her true burning fire is for someone else."

"Dudley you are too funny, I've never heard anyone put crazed sex in that context. Obviously you have done something for her to continue calling?"
"Let me clue you in without calling any names; but if you breathe a word to a soul rest assured our business transaction is off!"

"You have my word, not even Courtney will hear an ounce." A promise is a comfort to a fool, but in this case a deceptive snake.

"This female let's name her Delilah, she has been eluding herself, and for years infatuates over a mutual friend who in turn only sees her as street access. Believe me driving on her lane is like an open house party, which makes it hard to keep count of how many heads. And I use heads figuratively, for she's known for giving great ones."

"Wow!" I responded shockingly so as to keep up appearances; Angela has really made a name for herself, how low and stupid of her not to mention disgusting. She refuses to listen ever since school days, Angela always takes compliments about her skillful turns and twists as a means to share with men for material gains. All I've told her to value the kitty, pump some breaks; she continues to run herself to the ground. Deaf ears, so however she's being classed, that's her doing. Guess I need her to stay far away from Courtney, because I will do her worse than Tania did some months ago at Peppers.

"I myself was given access, as well as my friend who isn't aware of my involvement with her on that level. Needless to say Delilah got pregnant, she called me up and said that he was the father for a fact and needed my help to convince him. She knew very well my friend was separated from his

wife at the time she gave him access, if you ask me playing games to embarrass the wife."

"This all sounds like some soaps or television series, so why is she still calling you? Didn't she dig her claws into this man by having his baby?"

"Not quite, he actually reconciled with his wife during the pregnancy, but my friend never told his wife therefore things got ugly. It was like a threesome gone bad, real bad. After the baby was born my friend questioned the paternity and demanded a test, naturally Delilah refused and threw a fit. Not sure if she was hiding something, but at that time I became nervous, I damn near panicked it's a wonder I didn't have a heart attack. At that point of her refusal I thought to myself if this child is mine and this would cost me a great deal of unnecessary drama."

"Oh wow Dudley talk about some real life drama! I normally read about this from women of a lower standard. I've noticed the type of women who throw themselves at our Cricketers, usually girls with some decent upbringing, not necessarily an easy freeway chick from the bottom of the barrel. So what do you plan to do next? You cannot continue to ignore her calls; this might lead her to blackmail and or other desperate measures."

"You do have a point Marsha, but when I tell you she's a nut I'm not too sure a shrink can undo the knot that has her brains tied up. Delilah is bent on destroying my friend's wife perfect world; she's so jealous it sickens my stomach."
"Whose child is it though?" I asked, since this seems to be some mystery. "Perhaps the reason she's calling is to tell you that you are indeed the father."

"I must agree with you, but my six senses tells me she is trying to cook up some scheme. Reason being the baby died almost immediately after giving birth, so there is no need to call me like a serial stalker."

"What! The baby died? How comes?"

"Wish I could give you details, but I am not a Doctor. One thing I know for sure my friend and myself wants nothing to do with her."

"Well this is plenty to digest, so here what take a look at this proposal with your attorney. I am leaving first thing in the morning for Florida; I am scheduled to return to Jamaica three weeks from today. At that point I should have more investors and a closer timeline to know of an exact start date for this project."

"Fair enough, and remember not a word." He made certain to remind me of my promise to him.

"There's no need to worry Dudley, I've got you this is story is safe."

Tania
Signatures Please

"Sister dear let's go, it wouldn't look good being late for…What's wrong Tania? She asked barging in my bedroom.

"I can't believe my marriage will be over today, am I doing the right thing Sis?" I was in tears, a lifelong commitment to a man I've loved for years was about to end. For months Brian played hardball and suddenly 48 hours ago to be exact he called for an emergency resolution to dissolve our marriage. Jackie my rock since Brian and I separated came in the room comforting me. I've been tough months now keeping up appearances as the victim, deep down it hurts I'm losing my B, my rock.

"You will be fine Sis, time will heal all wounds. One thing for sure I am not going anywhere."

"I know Jackie…But Brian is." The house phone rings, distracting me from saying how I truly feel. "Hello mother, Tania is fine just going through the motions. Let me call you back a little later."

My mother kept Brian Jr. instead of hiring a sitter for the day, besides I didn't want her at the final proceedings. There's no telling what she would say or do to Brian, mother was very angry at him; the boy she was happy to have in the family as a teenager broke her baby girl's heart. Mother loved Brian like a son. Believe me she has no room in her heart to forgive him; mother can be very mean and tough at times we tried reasoning with her telling her that Brian is the father of her grandchildren. It was like talking to the walls, no penetration only your words bouncing back to your ears.

I took a few minutes to refresh my make up, and made sure my clothes was intact. I looked good for almost 7 months, whatever emotions I felt or was feeling the baby reacted. He moved around like a miserable hamster, oh yes I am having another boy. So picture me in couple months running around this house chasing to overly active boys. After this one definitely no more, it was never my intention to become a single parent. Not knocking it, just makes life easier when children grow up with both parents in the household.

"You look beautiful Tania, glowing and all. Brian is a fool and will always be one, he will regret all he did to you, trust my words." Jackie must have had some bitter grape juice this morning for her to say this; she has always been a Brian Lane fan from jump street.

"I see he's on your shit list now huh?" We both burst out laughing as we walked to the car. The attorney's office was only 20 minutes away, and I just had to face the reality, in a matter of hours I will be a single lady who is about to endure labor pains plus more heart ache.

"Tania, come here for a minute." My attorney Mr. Cleaners signaled me to step aside and away from eavesdropping ears.

"Is everything alright?" I asked as I glanced at my watch, we were scheduled to begin in 10 minutes, 10AM to be frank.

"Oh yes! Brian has agreed to most of your terms." His phone vibrated, interrupting us leaving an incomplete conversation that are suspenseful and can be very annoying.

"What does he want?" I whispered leaning close into his space, I was eager to hear what Brian was bargaining for, and basically telling Mr. Cleaners to get off the bloody phone and pay attention to me.

"He wants joint custody and alternate Holidays with the children." Leave it to a man to use his children as a pawn. Brian's life has become very unpredictable and I didn't want my kids to be around him, they need stability. Tossing them to and fro at either mother's or Jackie's house wasn't helping their growth and development already.

"Give me a few; I need to talk this over briefly with my sister."

"Sure, listen you can ask the Judge for more time, since Brian requested a speedy resolution after dragging his feet for months." He informed me. I felt the tears running down my cheeks ruining my make up once again.

"Tania what's wrong now?" Jackie was shaking, nervous as I searched for words that were unable to come out.

"He wants joint custody, basically in order to give me the money I deserve."

"Well Sis, that's not bad. Look on the brighter side he could have continued to dispute the terms and even offer less or ask for full custody. Remember he has a stronger earning power than you. Giving his connections things could go in his favor as well. Tania you are not losing your kids, just sharing under court a guideline that's not bad at all."

"I wanted to hurt him Jackie by taking the kids away from him. Letting Brian feel the pain he has put me through."

"As much as I don't care for him at this moment, that reason my sister doesn't make sense. It cannot erase what happened, nor will it stop the pain; if anything it will prolong it and spill over to the kids. They never asked for two bitter spiteful parents; both of you are responsible to grow them in a loving, and supportive environment." I held my sister tight, knowing she made sense; I was truly being spiteful and selfish.

"Jackie you are right, I will concede to his offer." Sobbing and trembling with mixed emotions I let go of my darling sweet sister.

"Dry your face; be strong for yourself and the kids. Walk in that conference room a winner and not a loser. Today is a new beginning, a chance to start over alone with great confidence, be that sassy, brave and determined little sister I have known all my life!"

Words have one of two effects, they either sink you or help lift you up; Jackie's did make me able to at least walked calmly into the room. Already sitting on one side of the table was Brian and his Attorney. He was beaming handsomely, looking so sexy and edible, why on earth was I thinking about sex? I'm pregnant for goodness sake, regardless of the fact; Brian had that affect on me, that strong animalistic sex craving desire to have him.

You could hear a pin drop, total silence as I sat slowly. I felt Brian's eyes watching me, so I looked at him; his eyes were either red from lack of sleep or from crying in pain. A grown macho man like him crying, I cannot even picture that.

"All stand as Judge Kelly presides." The clerk yelled, although we weren't in a courtroom we had to adhere to its formalities.

"Lane verses Lane, docket number 5689CEF." The clerk made reference to our case number, making it very clear as to who was sitting in front of the Judge and that he too had the correct documents at the forefront of his files.

"Have the parties in question come to a mutual agreement?" Judge Kelly asked, looking through her tiny, but yet thick reading glasses. She was mean; most regard her as an iron horse. The harder you rider her, the more pain your buttocks will feel or damn near bleed from the decisions she makes during a hearing. I hope she doesn't reduce the monthly payments, seeing that I was responsible for bringing Patrick to video tape the brawl which has resulted in Brian suspension from the team. Which also affects his income, and only God knows if the local Cricket Clubs will give him a chance to play during their upcoming tournaments.

"Yes we have your Honor." Both our Attorney's answered at the same time, guess they are in sink like a clock, which is ironic that's how they are being paid, at the tick of a clock.

Meanwhile outside of the conference room Jackie phone rings. "Hello." She answered.

"Jackie, is it too late to stop the proceedings?" Marsha asked with an extremely stressed out tone.

"Who is this?" Jackie asked, she was getting defensive for all she knew it could have been a gossip reporter or blogger fishing for an inside scoop.

"It's me Marsha; I have some information that could possible save their marriage."

"Spear me the drama Marsha, what are you trying to prove now? Now that Tania refuses to have you in her circle, you're desperately a super heroine? Where were you when your BFF and Brian were bundled up under the sheets?"

"Believe me I know I deserve that and even worse, but you have to listen to me Jackie; Angela is not alone in this web of deceit. Do you remember Brian's friend Dudley?"

"Yes I do, what does he have to do with anything?"

"I will reveal everything soon, meet me at..."

"Marsha I am not getting involve, especially with you and the likes of Angela. Leave me and my sister alone; she has been through enough already."

"Jackie hear me out, the dancehall artiste Tommy Lee describes himself as a demon right? Well Dudley is the father of them all, he's demonic, manipulative, not to mention arrogant to a point of utter disgust."

"Mr. Lane any final words before I make my ruling?" The Judge asked patiently.

"No your Honor." He answered like a rehearsed coward.

"What about you Mrs. Lane? I paused, gulped for a few minutes. Absolutely no words could come from my mouth, and then finally I was shock to hear my own voice.

"No your Honor, I have nothing further to add."

"Have a glass of water Mrs. Lane, take your time if you need to, you are obviously the victim here."

"Thanks you're Honor, but I am fine." I too was a coward.

"Well before I give my ruling let me address the parties. Mr. Lane in the future please to keep your pants, shorts a matter of fact all lower body garments on! If you were to remarry only your wife, the only other person the courts acknowledge as a complete union in a marriage is allowed to and is entitled to you have her way with your bodily parts. To put it across nicely, cheating and allowing a woman from easy access street into your marriage was a poor judgment on your part. Do you understand me?" She paused for a minute, drank from her Judge Judy commemorative coffee cup.

"As for you Mrs. Lane, never bring a camera to a cat fight. The media has no regard for your emotions because you didn't have for yourself. Do understand I was sitting where you are now, and went through your pain, so I can certainly relate. I will advice you as well, that in the future please walk away, never allow yourself to stoop lower. Trash belongs at street level, class yourself like a high rise building standing above and yet looking down at meaningless cheap access filth."
Both Attorney's were dumb founded, I too was shocked at her bluntness she doesn't mince her words. We all sat quietly as the Judge reviewed our file, not showing much emotion she glanced at the pages.

"Ok I have taken a number of facts into consideration, and will make amendments. I hereby grant full custody to Mrs. Lane. Raising two children in this present economy is more than overbearing so I motion to increase monthly payments by a 30%..."

"Your honor may I object?" Brian's Attorney interrupted her, bad move on his part iron judge was ruling in my favor. For this I love her!

"No, for if you do I will increase it to 50% now let me finish; once Mrs. Lane remarries she automatically doesn't get alimony. So therefore take my advice, have your kids, work on getting your life back in order, and I will stress this point. Take as long as you need to, same lengthy time frame applies to dating another man, far much less marry. Do you hear and understand me?"

"Yes Judge." I answered like a toddler in kindergarten.

"Good, I will have the clerk make the necessary changes to reflect my ruling and the documents should be ready in 45 minutes to be signed by both parties and their Attorney. You all are dismiss, and see you back here in 45 minutes."

I sat still glued to my seat, this was more than what I was expecting, however Brian looked as though a train ran over him, leaving him spineless, or in this case almost penniless.

"Tania are you ok? Do you need help to get up?" My Attorney asked.

"Yes I am fine, just need a minute to process all this information." Of course I lied, I was feeling the baby move, and wanted to share this moment with Brian who was two steps from existing through the door."

"Brian." I called out to him. "Come here for a second." He walked over to me pulled up the chair and sat next to me.

"What's happen Tania?" He asked so calm, cool and collective, our eyes were locked red from both tears and stress.

"Feel your son moving, he has been active all morning." There was a half of a smile from his face. I could tell deep down he was excited, Brian never had this opportunity with Little B.

"So it's another boy?" He asked.

"Yes another miniature you, I mean it in a good sense B I'm not trying to insult you by any means."

"T, I was thinking if you would like I can stay with you until your due date? Or come stay with me, it's not good for you to be alone in the apartment."

"You do have a point, but no thanks. If it does come down to it, I will stay with either mother or Jackie. I'm not at all sure that you have experience with labor contractions, you might run instead of carrying me to the hospital." We both shared a laugh.

Now this was a Kodak moment, however there weren't any cameras. Jackie would love to see us, not fighting but bonding for the sake of our baby.

"I see you two didn't bother to leave. It's always good when divorce couples get along." Judge Kelly said, with a little relief in her voice, guess she was happy there wasn't any tension between us, for the baby's sake that is.

"Well please get back to your respective seats, as I am about to finalize this proceeding. Clerk please tell their Attorney's we are ready."

That was it, the end! Brian and I are officially unmarried! Please don't cut me with a knife, because I am bleeding inside out.

"Sister dear, how did it go?" Jackie asked as soon I exited the conference room.

"Better than expected, Judge Kelly had compassion towards me and basically ruled more in my favor. Brian has to pay 30% more than what I had initially asked for."

"Great news Tania, this is just perfect! Best thing that could happen during all this chaos. By the way are we going to mothers or your place to celebrate?"

"I'm not feeling so hot Jackie, but you know mother will ring our necks if we didn't stop by, besides I need to see little B."

"You do have a point there Tania, plus I am starving for some home cook stew peas, our favorite."

"What? You better gas it to Portmore sis, that pot has our name on it!" We laughed like two silly school girls. I needed it to cheer up from the past two years of Brian Lane heartache.

***

"Bloody Mary-Jane!" Jackie yelled after reading her text message.,

"What's wrong now?" I asked she very seldom she uses that expression, so something must have bugged her stew peas run, actually our stew peas run.

"Ok I know the store, but why do you have to go now? My mouth real watering for some stew peas lady it better be quick."

"Long story Tania, I promise you our stews peas will not get cold."

So here we are, parked in the car lot, it's almost 1PM and this shopping center is ram packed. I wonder what's going on at Saudi Boutique, let me get out the car since Jackie is in the book store talking on her phone and not even paying attention to me. Wait there a minute, was I seeing right? That's Brian's red X5, is he following us? Let me dodge and hide myself, well at least try to hide this bump. He is sitting there talking on his cell, I wonder with whom? Jackie is on her phone, and so is he; hope this isn't some kind of conspiracy. Five minutes passed and he is still on his phone, ok I cannot continue to hide out here so let me just walk to the Boutique and see what sales they are having.

Wow! Some really great items on sale today, just cannot try them on. Oh Gees this baby stomach has two more months or there about; then it's back to my sexy dresses and pants. However it doesn't hurt to browse around, or better yet get some accessories. Perhaps a few beaded jewelry, oh yes I saw that large wood bracelets in a Fashion Magazine recently! Luckily I brought my credit card, and now that I am single there is no need to explain as to why I went shopping!

"Hello Jackie dearest, thought you were hungry for mother's stew peas and white rice? But here you are talking on your phone in this beautiful book store."

"Yeah I know but the parties are running late, a last minute meeting of the brains."

"Jacks guess who is sitting in the parking lot, well actually in his car doing surveillance or just stalking us I think. Guess who?"

"I am guessing the man from Chain Saw." There we go again laughing like two silly girls.

"No smart pants, Brian." For some reason Jackie didn't react surprised, she immediately started

texting. I am beginning to wonder what all these
James Bond secret motions are about. Since she
was busy I decided to walk around the store,
searching for more baby books, as if I didn't have
two boxes at home filled with Little B's collection.
Oh these are some nice children's books and tapes
for Little B and his brother, credit card in hand so I
will be buying them. Besides shopping is good for a
newly divorced woman, a form of guilt therapy;
food isn't an option so SHOPPING it is!

Why is it Brian, Jackie and Marsha sitting together?
I left Jacks busy texting, her thoughts distance,
thought this was a business meeting, a real quick
one at that.

"What the hell is going on here?"

"Tania, please just sit and don't cause a scene. This
isn't an intervention, just an opportunity to expose
a deadly poisonous snake." Marsh explained, as if I
really care for anything she says, seeing her makes
me sick.

"So who is this snake Marsha, I thought your
bleached skinned friend Angela was it." I asked, not
so politely.

"Sis, just sit down and relax, remember your
condition, the baby ok so chill." Now Jackie, no
miss pretender has something to say. Brian sat in
total silence, with a very calm cool demeanor. I am
not sure how Jackie and Marsha were able to
convince him to be here, to listen to God knows
what drama. We just ended one drama couple
hours ago, now another is about to unfold.

"Ok you all have my attention, reluctantly however I will listen."

"Good. I recorded a conversation I had with Dudley." Marsha said very slowly as if she was choosing her words carefully.

"Wait, you said Dudley?" I asked rolling my eyes, and then looked into Jackie's eyes. She was the only person I told what Dudley did to me before I got married to Brian.

"Marsha, are you crazy? Dudley is a known womanizer, not a gossip mole. Come on do better than this." Mr. Brian said defending his immoral friend. Marsha sure had my attention; Dudley rubbed me bad from day one.

"Be quiet Brian and just listen to the tape." Marsha became annoyed; she pressed the play button and unfolded what no one expected but; **The Truth!**

After all the truth came out, yes, well no because I have something to share with Brian right here, right now. Then again Brian looked so steamed with rage, I mean if Dudley were to walk into the store it would immediately become a Mike Tyson vs. Evander Holyfield fight.

"Brian, please listen to me. There is more that's not on that tape." Both Marsha and Jackie looked at me as if I was crazy.

"What? You have secrets too?" Marsha asked surprised.

"I am afraid I do, should have told you long time ago, but he threatened to break us up. Well technically he did, that day on the verandah when he told you a lie about me leaving the Cricket Wives Club fundraiser with another man. Planting seeds of doubt about little B's paternity."

"Tania you are making partial sense here, tell me from the beginning how did you get involve with Dudley to the point of keeping secrets from me."

I started from that night, and gave Brian a complete breakdown step by step recount of what his dear old friend Dudley did. When I was finished Jackie backed me up with what took place the day after, how she had to come and get me from work, because I was lost, walking around like a zombie. Brian looked away from me, he could face me. He was both upset and shocked to hear this after divorcing the woman he loves. He now realized how much of a fool he was, the biggest mistake he could have done in his life. It wasn't about just sleeping with Angela, he trusted Dudley, a loyalty among men a bond now broken.

"In life…you can and will never know a person true color until it's very late." That's all he said, and walked away and not once did he look at me.

Tania
Dear Diary

Dear diary, today I will write to you as Tania
Watson, no longer am I Mrs. Lane. We finalized the
divorce this morning, and something else profound
happened as well, which I will share in a second. First there
is a very beautiful love song from the 'Waiting to Exhale'
album that I am feeling the words to now; *Why does it hurt
so bad? Why do I feel so sad? Thought I was over you, but I am still
crying because I still love you.'* Our divorce proceedings went
better than expected, the only emotional surprise Brian and
I had was a truth intervention, or should I rephrase it, a
truth revelation.

We all knew Angela was an individual with issues,
and that she was determined to be with Brian just to hurt
me. Honestly no one else knew the level of deceit Dudley
would stoop to, and on the surface pretending to be Brian's
best buddy. When the entire truth as we heard on the audio
recorder came out, you should have seen the shock, disgust
and pain on Brian's face. So many secrets, the emotional
truth that caused our marriage to deteriorate, as I sit here I
wonder if I was too quick to end things or should I at least
had tried counseling.

Guilt is now creeping in, it's not easy being pregnant, heartbroken, and knowing I played a hand in this dominos ripple effect. Why am I here writing when I should be praying, praying for forgiveness and peace between Brian and I. During our marriage Brian was hilarious with his **Pum Pum Law and Order** looking back now that night was indeed the best! Well it's good therapy to reflect on the best time of our union, trust me it helps.

Only pain and agony is in this house, let me go to sleep, sleep in my empty bed. Until my next entry, the only thing I can do is pray.

Broken
My heart is broken, how do I make it become whole again?
When my subconscious thoughts are still of you.
Many will come and go but will never replace you…you are the one.

Angela
Kitty's Physical Therapy

Obviously my counselor is attractive, but after sitting in his office waiting for him to walk in, and fix my head straight from Brian's love cloud to his sexiness. My lust levels turned up 200 degrees when my eyes were blessed, teased and became hungry, lips watering all four of them, as my counselor general bulge outweighed Brian's by far. I was shock at his pants, instead of looking at him; I looked at his candy cane treat, based on the look of things it sure will be sweet for all my lips to savor. So funny but it were as though his candy cane sensed my presence, and stood firm and for some reason a tent was pitched.

Not all men are equal, some pleased while other teased. My counselor, whose name is actually Milford Strokes or Ital Strokes for a sexier purpose, had me doing airplanes, helicopter and hand back crawling up the walls. Shit his girth was thick as thieves, a really non-condom sized dick if you should asked me.

Oh I love my sexy tightness as I sit on this toilet preparing, and using lavender scented kitty wash fragrance. Refreshing kitty for round two with the counselor, fresh and clean is how I love to serve it. After seeing his bulge yesterday, tight kitty needed him to loosen up her wet entry and I am glad he came. His ice-cream fountain or whatever your pet name or phrase might be, my mouth had tasted something great! Sorry if you cannot stomach reading this, but that's how I love it, creamy and thick.

"Angela my tight gymnast, what's taking you so long with the kitty Empress? He yelled from the bedroom.

"Give me a few." I answered as I refreshed and dried kitty, a man like him loves dried meat before he eats. Well he is a vegetarian so it's more like dried fruits. This rebound sex, kitty's therapy, or hardcore batting, licking, sticking, just whatever you want to call it. My counselor general is about to have my fruit or red cherry apple whichever name suits you again, and will most certainly eat well or even better than the first round.

Brain failed in comparison, I remember the first time he went down south, OMG! He tickled me, I had to teach him. I just bet Tania never had him do her, well he did mention that she annoyed him about eating her and he never gave in. If you ask me Brian was confused, why eat me and not your precious wife? That goes to show how some men are flip flops, drag slippers. Yeah she was wife but funny enough I had one up on her blind ass, a matter of fact two. My pregnancy hit her like a blind bat flying into a tree trunk.

"Angie what you doing?" he slowly opened the door, sticking his head in the bathroom butt naked.

"Sitting on the toilet, come over here." He walked towards me, swinging his dingdong. As he stood in front of me I held his piece in my mouth while using my hands to rub his balls.

"Empress go easy with the dread." He said with a huge smirk on his face. I going to see how long before his knees buckle. 10-15 minutes, I had longevity, air pocket lips and jaws. I *Worked It* like the title of Missy Elliot hit song. My Ital Strokes will never leave my bedside after I am done with him tonight, up next I will show him some rodeo tricks.

Give it to me one more time, that's the hook to the song right? Ital Strokes gave it to me five times more in total and each time stronger than before my poor kitty was worked out to the core. The dread popped it down, leaving no more red, shoot this was the best strokes I ever had in my life. One thing for sure, never underestimate a dread and his way of life, talk about stamina. According to him his diet and chimney herbs makes him strong and ready.

"Empress, you don't need to look for a real man anymore. I am here to rock and toss your boat. I want to love you and care for you like an Empress in my world."

"I am sensing there is a BUT?" I had an idea where he was going with this.

"There is no but, just a mental transformation and realization of self. As my Empress you are expected to act and dress like one, likewise it's my duty to treat you as such."

"Go on; please list what I need to do." I asked very intrigued and open to being his.

"It's not what you need to do; it's more along the lines of you knowing where you are in Jah world. Recognizing your roots, and embracing your natural form."

After one night this man wanted me in his world? Guess I should have held back all the tricks instead of giving him all in one night. Perhaps I should just stop feeling regrets and listen to his way of life? One thing for sure I will never let go of his *Ital Strokes*.

"You will be fulfilled in my world and overstand yourself!" His after sex pillow talk, or debate was an eye opener and I welcome his insights. On a professional level he knew me as a client needing help. Now I was letting him into my inner walls, and just perhaps my heart for a change. God knows I needed it.

Speaking of change, I got a text message informing me that Brian and Tania are dried toast; their buttering loving romance is officially over. Too bad for her, as mine is now beginning, I will be more than a man's wife, I will be an Empress!

Tania
Burning Guilt

Talk about love, talk about forever baby when you talk about us. Oh I so wish the words to this love song by Michael Bolton rang true reality in my life right now. God why on earth am I so confused? Men always say women are confused; we act on emotions and not use concise facts before making any decisions for the most part. I feel like crap! Brian was furious to say the very least, after learning the truth about Dudley. I am guilty as charged for keeping this secret. I've called, sent text messages for three days, still he fails to respond. God damn it I'm pregnant and going through all this stress! Being alone is not a good thing. Again, why me God? Why us? Why did the perfect couple split? Did I rush the divorce? Should I have sought counseling? Day 3 after the fact of our inked signature of the divorce decree, I want a refund, wait, what am I saying? I want my union back, and our marriage reinstated. Brian Christopher Lane is my world; there was no way I could ever deny this fact.

Saturday morning, so beautiful outside looking out the window of my small bedroom, seems ever smaller without both my men here. Salty tear runs drops down my face, the pain is unbearable, unspeakable, and unforgettable. 'Breathe Tania Watson, take deep breathes.' I had to say to my lonesome self in front of a mirror. 'You will be just fine Tania, have your baby and get back on track.' It didn't matter what I said to myself, misery was still in my head. What the hell to do? I am miserable, fat due to being pregnant, unable to move around quickly, not to mention not feeling beautiful and sexy. What am I saying and actually doing to my mental state of mind? I can always call my dearest sister Jackie and bore her with tearful telephone conversations. Dialing up one Jackie Watson...

"Jackie I need you now." My usual begging for affection, attention or whatever, I truly have become needy, oh well that's what sisters are there for. Tears in my eyes, my body and spirit in complete grief and agony over the loss of a love one; in my mind I was a never ending funeral service. Weeping, mourning, black, purple, dark, dampened, and raining depressing tears, in a nutshell this was now my world.

"Tania Watson what's wrong now? You've made your bed so stay still and give yourself time to heal. Stop worrying about him!" Jackie's tone was one of tough love.

"Jacks one thing for certain, Brian Lane loves me. *If only I had trust and believed in our love we both wouldn't be hurting now.*"

"Well Tania you need therapy and I am not certified. Glad you are recognizing the truth about how you feel, but I cannot stop my life to fix yours. As for you not hearing from him, check the sports news sister dear. He is off to Trinidad playing a tournament this weekend."

As his wife I would have already known this information, but now it as if I am a stranger. Just counting the days till I pop this child out, would like for him to be at the Hospital to witness the birth of his son. We haven't discussed a name, so much tension we haven't had time to talk about what was important. Our baby would come into this world...let me not even entertain any sort of negativity when it comes to my children, not one ounce.

"Jacks, I love you sis. I will call you later."

Brian
Sweet Trinidad Ladies

When a man loves a woman, he has to know when to let her go; and if she is meant for you, she will come back. Tania wanted a divorce, so I gave her what she asked for, or bloody near demanded. I am hurting too, not only have I lost her, but also what I had in mind for our future. Tania and our children means the world to me just needed the opportunity to show her that I was willing to change.

Women tend to think we don't feel pain, as if they are the only ones who cry over a broken heart. So unbelievable and ridiculous and nothing we do is enough, then why bother, I often ask myself. Why do I even bother to try? Tania annoyed the hell out of me about what I did, from what I didn't do. It became too unbearable; her thoughts were all over the place, the funny thing is she knows very well she wants to be with me. Women are a handful, and a pain in the butt.

You know what really hurts me right now? She is calling me constantly after getting the divorce, and feeling guilty about what she did with Dudley. Or should I say what he did to her. Living a life of lies, a house of crumbling cards is just like being a joker in a pack. I will confront Dudley, but right now cricket business comes first. As you know I have a huge child support and alimony to pay. I will not subject myself to further humiliation by physically attacking him. It will only result in media frenzy. Been there not going back!

Well since I am a free man, here in Trinidad with more than a handful of beautiful Indian women who love Cricket and not to mention the players. I will be having a ball, and sharing a few balls with them. I am not saying they are easy birds, they know exactly what the deal is, no strings attached we are only enjoying each other's company. Their spirit is more along what I am looking for right now, having fun. I met one some weeks ago, pretty young lady, Donna Kusum she turns up the heat.

"I hope you staying longer than 5 days Brian?" She asked, lying next to me on this King sized bed.

"Why Donna, for what reason do you need more of me?" I asked with a big smile, she wanted more of this Jamaican groove. I was rubbing her plumped backside as she rolls away from me, sticking her naked soft butt for me to notice she wanted more of what Tania is missing. Her skin was so soft and spotless, her body and breasts were like a Barbie. Oh yeah, I am a real Star Boy!

"It would be my pleasure to take you around the country side, our island is just as beautiful as Jamaica, or even more if you ask me." Donna was being patriotic to her country, this was understandable.

"Really now, just remember we carry big things, or bigger things! I don't need to see the rest of the island when I already have a beautiful sculpture like you." That's what it took to get her all worked up and ready for another challenging round. How the phrase went again? *Cricket, wicket he knows how to stick it.* I know how to stick it right down Donnas' middle for certain.

"Brian Lane I must agree you are big, might not be bigger, than a bushman from the deep hills of TT, but since we Trini women are sweeter than a yardie let me share some sweets with you again…" Donna climbed up and rode this Jamaican stiff shift like a real jockey, Tania has nothing on her, Donna could teach her a few tricks. The only thing Tania has is my heart, but you know I will keep Donna as my main Trini-Lady and fly her to Jamaica if needs be.

Yes man, I need to scout a new chick in England, Guyana or even Barbados, listen I am free, single and disengaged, they call me Star Boy for a reason might as well I live it up.

Believe me when I tell you Donna was a great gym instructor, although the team had couple hours of training each day, her work out were more impactful, she had a wire waist line. Sweet, sweet Donna, a very sweet Trini-Ting.

"Swing, man, open the door I know you are in there getting your shine." Dudley, that son of a bitch wasn't getting my signal, guess his antenna malfunctioning. I want nothing to do with him; he has tried talking to me a few times already, and each time I ignore him. This man just nuff and full of crap like a crab.

"Dudley what do you want from me? Boss easy and bounce I'm not in the talking mood right now." I yelled, this man was disturbing my workout. I know I need to confront him, just not right now.

Tania Watson shows up on my cell-phone screen, she is not getting the picture I've been ignoring her calls;

and now that the tables turn she wants to talk, a typical woman so emotionally confused.

"Tania what can I do for you? You wanted a divorce; I signed the papers, why are you calling my phone like a bill collector? Are you in labor?"

"Might as well I was in labor! Brian you have all right to be upset, I get that, but to be so nasty!"

"Listen I am here chilling with my girl Donna, so make it fast or hang up." I didn't mean to hurt Tania's feelings but I need my space, and she needs to get a grip.

"Brian Lane, your shower ready baby." Donna yelled from the bathroom, what a man to do when a hot treat is in the building. Donna is making me feel like Trinidad is my true birthplace; having her every night will be very nice indeed.

"Ok Brian, I hear her, go ahead have fun…you will never change, and to think you loved me…" I could hear the pain in her voice, she was hurt. Too bad, I need to live in my moment now; I am a man with needs.

The only thing I could possible do after hearing Tania's voice was to continue shutting her out my thoughts. I need to feel like a man, and not like a used potato chip bag. Her constant nagging and negative comments only diminishes my manhood.

Oh Donna I am ready sweet-ting.!" I tell you the truth I had the best drop soap session ever.

Tania
Next in Line

I feel like a superwoman, hence the reason I am here in the supermarket with a due date of any minute now. Call me crazy, or plain out right stubborn, I was craving for stew peas and my kitchen cupboard was lacking a major ingredient. Go figure, red peas Thursday's are usually my stew peas day, and for the past month I haven't been able to cook pot. My body felt fine, no pains just this little man kicking last night, and now he seems to be sleeping or taking a rest. This giving me the quick I need second to run do my supermarket shopping and then chill for the remaining day.

Walking up and down these aisles looking for a list of other things to purchase, just in case I might need them instead of running back here walking or wobbling like a duck. In my mind I was looking like a busted pregnant woman, excess weight in my face, swollen ankle at nights. I don't know but baby number two wasn't making me look nor feel sexy at all.

"Girl do I have some news for you!" I heard a female voice saying to someone from another aisle. Not being able to see who she is, I decided to listen.

"Do you remember the Cricketer whose wife beat up the pregnant mistress?" she further informed her gossip partner on her cell. "She is in the supermarket looking all depressed, and her body was like an oversized whale pregnant with triplets!" The gossiper informed her listening partner.

This made me very curious to see who the hell she is. Following her voice I wobbled to where she was. You should have seen the mouth opening expression on her face as I snuck up behind her; as she continued giving her caller friend details as to what I was wearing. I guess she was either star struck or plain out right jealous; and I could see why this dwarf should be jealous.

Her dwarf frame was unattractive, coupling with poor taste in attire. Like seriously, who wears tie and die jeans in the 23rd century? She had no breast, a serious turnoff for most men, if not all men. Men love breast, it's like mother's milk in the bedroom, shoot I could give her some of my 44DD. Looking her dead in the face I wanted to slap the bad breathe down her throat as it contaminated the air that good people in the world had to suffer smelling.

"Get a life, and while you are at it get some height and a breast job!" I told her my mind, this trash bucket or dumpster is more like it, seeing her height was comparable to that Government free garbage bin on the sidewalks. My baby was kidding, as if he too was upset and wanting to fight for his mother. Walking away heading to the cashier, I was fuming with rage; I wanted to mop her on aisle 6. But I couldn't, I really couldn't giving my present condition.

"Next in line to register 7 please." I heard the cashier said out loud but it wasn't registering that she was talking to me. Another customer tapped my shoulder; bringing me to the surface of present time. For a second I reflected on the fight with Angela, and what I wanted to do this dwarf. God I need you to take this anger away from me, I cannot blame people for gossiping about me, I cannot blame someone else for this sharp pain I am feeling.

"Oh, someone please call the ambulance! My water broke!" I yelled as I walked up to Susie-B's cash register. The stress from the argument forced this little boy out. Again where is my absentee baby father when I need him!

Tania
New broom-Old broom

Two years later with two hyperactive kids, Brian
Lane Jr. also known as BJ since he was growing into big
brotherhood. Second was my now new baby boy of 2 years
Christopher Justine Lane, aka CJ. These two were a riot all
day every day; I thought I wouldn't have time for myself
much less a relationship. However a man, yes a man sure
got my attention and made all my Brian Lane love thoughts
vanish. Derrick Jones, Jackie's nicknamed him 'The
Magician'. Reason being, as Derrick grew on me almost
instantly, Brian Lane who? Brain Lane was history. Well for
the most part, I have two kids for him so they were the
only reminder.

An older man, whose experience in relationship
superseded mine. I had only been with Brian all my 20 plus
years on earth. How do I describe Derrick Jones? His
money and family ties, who wasn't too keen about having
me in their close family knot. Giving my public
embarrassing, disgraceful divorce; this was not a situation
or attention they welcomed into their powerful, elite,
socialite circle. I was immediately looked down upon by the
women in his family especially.

The first time I met his family was at a reunion two
years ago, and believe me it was very nerve wrecking.
Between his mother and four Aunts, i wasn't sure who
were more disgusting with slight insults and unwelcomed
questions. I felt like a criminal in an interrogation room..

Jackie described them as animalistic monsters on two legs, the only thing human were their DD's cup size breast. Who knows they could be FF's, with all that money, a having breast surgery shouldn't be a huge dent in their accounts. Good thing Jacks came with me, yes my sister dearest was by my side, she and I have weathered many storm, and this one was just another of many more to come.

"So nice to finally meet you Tina, or is Tania? I can't seem to keep up with Derrick's friends of late, blame it on old age." His mother greeted me with a mischievous smile. Her statement was plain out right intentional.

It was clear she had her guarded walls up, I would have to hire Bin Laden and his men to bomb that wall to pieces. But what am I saying, Bin Laden is dead…now who do I hire? Well I am going to be me, Tania Watson; no way will I take cover under Derrick's buttocks. She is and forever be his first lady, but I am here now, and darling I am not going anywhere.

"Well Derrick is a successful businessman with tons of friends and associates, so it's only natural it would be hard for you to keep up with names and faces. If my memory serves me right he father too was successful and had a handful of female relationships, back then you were much younger so I guess you started having memory loss since then." I shot back.

Mrs. Jones walked away so fast, you would think hurricane Gilbert gust through the room for a split second. She lucky I didn't slap my freshly manicured hands across her uptight fake society wrinkled face.

"Tania I guess it comes with the territory, your ex-husband had you in the same dilemma as Mr. Jones did with my sister. But let us move pass this cold block ice introduction and get to know each other for Derrick's sake. If you are going to be around for the long haul we have to get along like family." His Aunt Delores said in her sister's defense.

"I totally agree with you, but rest assured I will not be made a laughing stock, not by you nor any of his outside sexual interest."

Pow! More dose for her to swallow, if she thought her status as Derrick's mother and aunt will grant them permission to be unapologetic, and rude, they are all in for a stormy awakening. They all better think twice. I never had this reception with Brian's family, believe me, NEVER!

Poor Jackie, she was laughing the entire time. She later turned to me and said. "Little sister you did real well!"

From that day forward they were very careful when choosing their words, I had not time to complain to Derrick each time they got out of line; I handled it right then and there.

***

"BJ, hope you are dressed? Your father will be here any second." I yelled from my bedroom, BJ was going on 5 years old and acts so grown.

"Mom come here please." In his baby voice, that's the voice he uses to wrap me around his little fingers.

91

"What is it BJ" I asked, not leaving my room, not giving him control.

"I need your help mommy with my shoe lace." BJ was dressed, but couldn't tie his shoe lace properly if his life depended on it; or knowing him just wanted my undivided attention. I reluctantly went to my son's aide, and as I kneeled down to tie his lace, BJ stroked my hair.

"Mom." He said in a sneaky voice.

"Yes BJ, what can I do for you?"

"I want to go live with Daddy."

"What! Why Brian Lane Jr.?" BJ was spoiled but not to the point of knowing the difference between living here or there. I made certain there wasn't any tension at home or at his father's. So internally I asked myself where on earth this was coming from.

"Because I love my Daddy and like playing video games with him."

"That's not enough reason, besides CJ will miss you."
I was trying my best to show BJ that he is wanted here, and loved as well. I lift this 60lbs child and kissed his adorable cheeks. "Mommy wants you here BJ."

"Uncle Derrick can give you a new baby Mommy, and CJ can play with him." Holding back the tears, I never thought this day would come so soon. BJ loves his Dad, and idolized him to the core. I hugged and kissed him, I never wanted BJ to feel the strains of our divorce or discomfort of having a new partner.

"BJ I love you. Mommy loves you more than you can imagine, but when the time is right you can go live with your Daddy. But right now home is with me."

BJ is just like his father, very territorial since Derrick and I are engaged and living together he has been acting strange, not necessarily rude and outlandish, but more so withdrawn which is a trait is like his Dad. For the most part Derrick is very nice with him, well when I am around. Speaking of the devil, he now walks through BJ's room door.
"Hey son, are you ready for cricket camp?" Brian's voice was filled with excitement, naturally to have his son walking in his cricket footsteps only one other word to describe it, PROUD.

Derrick must had let Brian in, because I didn't even hear the door bell; to everyone's surprise they both got along and I couldn't ask for anything less. My children, my boys are going to have a peaceful family life, being divorced to Brian, and about to marry Derrick I wasn't allow the changes in my life disrupt their environment, I intend to create a very normal and loving atmosphere as possible.

"Brian we need to talk, are you free this Tuesday around 12pm?" I had to ask since he was so busy these days.

"I am not so sure, but will try to squeeze you in." Oh yes he had to answer with a certain air about him, he just had to let you know he was the hit factor in Cricket these days. Now that the board reinstated his position on the team, and his social life with team mates and women was on page 6 regularly party events. He was just where he wanted to be, in Brian Lane's world having the time of his life.

"You better make time! It's about BJ."

"Ok Boss Lady, since you are still my Queen, you run things." Shaking my head, Brian was just being fresh; I swear my engagement is eating him alive under false pretence. Mr. Great Pretender. Who left the same way he came in, quietly, and of course CJ was crying his eyes out for BJ.

"Don't cry munchkin, big brother BJ will be back. When you get older Daddy will take you along." I whispered in his tiny ears as I tickled his belly. Treating both of them equally can be a bit challenging.

Lord have mercy, what has become of Brian Lane, the Star Boy of West Indies Cricket? I can just imagine the number of wanna be Mrs. Lane coming in and out of his bedroom. Well as long as they are 500 feet away from my boys, I couldn't care less.

"What was that all about you wanting to talk with Brian?" Here comes Derrick, hope he was concerned and not jealous.

"BJ asked me to go live with him, and I need to know what's going on when they are together; wait a minute am I sensing a slight bit of jealousy?"

"No. not at all, is just that you didn't talk to me first like you use to."

"Oh, things happen and there is always a first time for everything." I had to answer him like that, OMG sometimes I think Derrick just don't understand or is not cut out to be in this divorce slash child custody situation. I love Derrick for obvious reasons; he caters to me a little more than Brian did during our marriage. He has great qualities, but I get the feeling he has been trying hard to fit in with the boys, as oppose to make it happen more organic.

"I think BJ should live with his Father, a boy needs his Dad to learn how to be a man."

"Derrick when I ask for your two senses, I will let you know ahead of time. My boys' welfare is my concern, not yours. They are young and impressionable, and if I don't create a normal living situation, they may just become an emotional time bomb. Kill me dead they are not going to have any emotional baggage thanks to either me or Brian!"

"So why bother have me in your life then? Why bother to wear my ring if I cannot voice my opinion? You over think this situation, holding on to your boys is the only thing I see you care about, I just hope that's all and you are not using them in hopes of getting back with your Star Boy."

"Tell you what Derrick the front door might be closed, but the day I open it and ask you to leave is the day you will know where you truly stand. Don't ever psychoanalyze my children's life."

"Tania let me leave; I will be at my place if you need me or when you calm down."

Derrick left, I was heated and in rage, again this temper of mine, but to really think about it, how dear him! Besides I could use the space, he needs to stay away for a few days. I will pack CJ's bag and drop him off at Mother's for the weekend, the next two nights I will chill with some wine and figure out my life with or without Derrick.

8:35AM, the boys were already out the door, BJ off to kindergarten and the other pre-k, while I had tons to do besides meeting Brian as scheduled for noon. I will just throw a skirt and Polo top on, we shouldn't take long talking about our son's welfare. Remember it's not just child support; it's about me giving up full custody after fighting hard for it.

Traffic was bumper to bumper, it's 11:35 I am 25 minutes away from Spices Jerk restaurant. Oh snap that's Brian calling me.
"Yes Brian, I know I might be late there is some much traffic here at the square." Not giving him an edge to talk, or question how far away I was from our meeting place.

"Tania, there is a change in plans."

"What? How could you do this to me? You had ample time to call and tell me something came up Brian!" I was pissed!

"If you would just give me a word in edge wise, and stop yapping those gums."

"Speak your mind Brian."

"Meet me at my house, the car battery died plus I think there might be some engine troubles."

"Battery, engine troubles, make up your mind Brian, you know I am pressed for time with the kids and picking them up from school."

"I know Tania, I am their Father, and oh my do you act like they are only yours, as though I didn't play a role in making them."

Tilsa C. Wright

"Brian, see you in thirty minutes at your place as you so wish." Damn Brian for not being more organized, and that's who BJ wants to live with. Frustration coming from all angles, first BJ, then Derrick now Brian and his star boy life attitude, Lord Father show me a sign please. It took me 40 minutes to get to Brian's; lunch traffic was a mess if you ask me too many cars on this tiny island, not enough streets, lane, avenues, and roads to accommodate them. But again we are living in the new day, where access to material things or luxury items is easy like 1, 2, 3. Just as long as I pick up the boys from school by 3PM, my mind will be at ease, need to spend at the most one hour at Brian's in order to accomplish this.

"Brian, let me just get straight to the point." I had no time to dance around the issue.

"What's wrong now Tania, for all the stress you putting me through?"

"Well for starters, what's going on when BJ is alone with you for the weekends?"

"Nothing out of the normal, a perfectly great father son relationship, we have fun, watch cartoons. Why?"

"For some reason he wants to make a big deal about living with you."

"Tania this means you need to address something on your end, because he is totally fine when with me."

"Kiss my ass Brian, not one damn thing is going on at my house. You have all the women in and out of here like a fudge shop, offering sweet joy ride."

97

"I see you are jealous, obviously you could use some good loving, to ease the tension right now." He said with a smirk.

"Don't you wish you could have some of this Brian, dream on, besides I am done with sharing the ride on your rollercoaster."

"On a more serious note though Tania, you have Derrick living with you, so what else do you expect? He is getting a little confuse calling him uncle, and seeing the two of you kissing and whatever. BJ did ask me why I am not kissing you if I am his Daddy as far as he knows mommy and daddy are supposed to be kissing, not uncle and mommy."

"Point taken Brian Lane, point very much so taken; so how do we handle this?"

"Well I propose he stays with me when I have time from tournaments, let's say for a two or three week time frame."

"No problem, just keep your sleazy women out of here!"

"Would you like something to drink, juice, coconut water…because you seem to be bent out of shape or lacking something to be so tense. You need to relax before you pop a vessel."

"I will pour myself what I want from the kitchen; don't want you slipping me a Mickey Mouse."

"Ha-ha, you too funny Tania, if I want you now I can have you, there's no need for me to do that. I know the buttons to press, remember I got the first code from 18."

"Once again Brian, kiss my ass." Oh bananas and cream, why did I say that? Brian got up from the living room and rushed to the kitchen, grabbing me around my waist, pin me against the counter.

"Now Brian you need to relax, you know I was only kidding around." He was in a zone, that zone was to have me right here and right now.

"Don't fight me Tania; let me remind you of what you use to have with me, the way I made you feel, your body responding to my thrust, my kiss, massaging those girls, and your centerpiece. Besides my bed is too big without you, two years and it feels bigger each day."

"Centerpiece, that's what you calling it now? You're bed too big, since when?"

"Hush and let me do what I do best for you, in a few you will know what's too big."

I instantly remembered Jah Cure song, 'Only You' for only Brian had the first sets of keys; or the Pum Pum Law and Order he alone came up with.

"B, we cannot do this, it's not right or fair to Derrick."

"We, what we? Forget about Derrick. You know I am the only one you love. Derrick cannot and will not replace me. So relax and enjoy what I am about to do. I see you not paying attention to my words, too big is Christopher Martin's new single. Let me play it for you, miss tightness."

I couldn't resist the truth; he had my panties wet, my knees weak, and my nipples hard, I was ready to receive his tools of trade. His larger than Derrick's tool of trade,

Brian had his hands up my mini skirt, pulling my panties down to my knees. Our eyes were locked; I was looking him dead in the eyes, yearning for his lips to be one with mine. He didn't care how this would play out, nor did I.

"I feel someone's juices are ready…Let's go into my room." I was lost for words as he kissed my neck, his former girls; picking up the boys was a distant memory all I know my body wanted to get plucked in a manner of speaking. Lying on his bed with my legs open wide effortlessly, and watching him undressing, had my mouth watered at his sexy chiseled body. Brian was HARD!

I couldn't wait for his penetration. Condom, no baby I only use that with Derrick as a premarital precaution, besides he was small and condoms fitted him perfectly he was nowhere close to Brian's length. Finding a condom size that would fit Brian was quite a challenge at times, anyways I wanted that rawness to fill the sides of my walls, that friction squeezing and gripping him tight. Using his mushroom head Brian slowly entered, fighting a bit, as the old saying goes, new broom sweep clean, but old broom knows all the corners. But in this case not only does Brian know the entire corners, his broom stick reached further.

"Brian, please take it easy, use some Vaseline if you need to, don't tear me up. I need to be able to walk out of here the same way I entered."

"Why you acting so scared? It's the same size, the size you use to love this. You have the natural tightness T, that's all." Brian telling me this made me even hotter, I couldn't wait to suck him after he comes. His strawberry, grape, flavored lollipop, delicious sweetness, my mouth was ready to please him.

"Oh B, that's it, right there baby. Oh Jesus help me!" This was the best backers in months, correction years, my favorite position. Brian had me twisting and turning on the bed like a spring chicken, we were trying to outdo each other. 20 minutes and he still didn't come.

"Brian, stop holding it, come baby." Anything to get him there, damn I forgot he had stamina for hours without end.

"Stay still, I coming just now." Yeah right, it took him another 10 minutes or so before he came, and mind you he never pulled out. Mr. Fertilizer just loves pumping his juices into the Law and Order tank.

"Brian may I go now?"

"Why?"

"I have to pick up the boys by 3…it's now 1:45 at least I think." I couldn't read the time clearly on his digital radio player.

"Just give me 5 more minutes."

"For what Brian, what now my body cannot take another round?"

"Don't worry Tania just know you are the only girl that can fit this, so come back up for me baby girl, let me feel the edges again, and again."

Five minutes seemed like 55, Brian was drunken by Christopher's song, he used lines to really get me wanting him, and to my absolute surprise Brian did the unimaginable. Lying on my back, he ate me for the first time; this Star Boy had my head in the galaxy…I saw stars, moon and all the planets. This was my first time, but obviously not his. Didn't matter though, he wasn't my husband anymore. We had a relapse of great sex and nothing more. OMG wish Derrick could be this bloody good! Yeah, yeah I know, I cannot have my cake and eat it, only in my world but not the real world. Derrick was a good man, the sex was 4 out of 10, but comparing him to Brian, well no comparison, Brian was a 30 tipped the scale and then some. Let me stop talking about scale, and figure out how to get to my boys school in time. Oh shit my panties were in a bunch, I was wet, slightly bruised, walking like fire was burning the hairs off my centerpiece…LOL Brian's new name for it.

"Mommy, you are here." That's my BJ, happy to see me, running towards me, wrapping his arms around my hips. "What took you so long Mommy?" Mr. Nosy, or Mr. Concern, whichever he was a handful, and often times acted like my boss.

"I went to meet your Daddy about you going to live with him." Well I find it hard to lie to my 5 year old who acted like 25.

Securing them into their car seats I was hoping they didn't smell their father on me. I didn't have time to jump in the shower before leaving, I felt good, but not clean being around others and smelling of Brian Lane. One thing for certain, I didn't have to worry about Derrick coming over tonight, for he was still upset, and trust me I wasn't going to call him over either. After what just happened between Brian and I, there was no way I could let him touch me. Brian left his huge size print; poor Derrick would be lost and swimming like a toddler. Not exactly the image I wanted to paint for you, but you sure get the drift, right?

I got the boys settled as soon as we got home; I quickly rushed to my bathroom and showered. I had to wash off Brian, but on the flipside my body enjoyed being with him, I felt awakened, revived, rejuvenated; it's been a really long day. Just a pity I couldn't call him over to spend the night, I would have loved to ride him like I use to, today's lunch quickie was an appetizer, I need him for main course and lots of desserts. Brian Christopher Lane, got me good today, he really did.

"Mommy, mommy here, take this." BJ ran into the room with the cordless phone. I didn't even hear it ring, that shows you how much Brian had my levels off.

"Hello." I said, after all there wasn't a name or number on the caller ID.

"It's your B, just calling to make sure you got the boys in time, and that you are okay with what happened today."

"The boys are fine. As for me, I am trying to wrap my thoughts as to what and why we did whatever today. But what else can I say, what's done is done, we have to move pass it."

"Easy for you to say Tania, I didn't plan to make love to you, I didn't plan to not have my car functioning in order to lure you into my bed. You know our sexual chemistry is potent to the point of burning up a lab."

"Brian I know this, but I rather not talk about it. I have to deal with a wedding in two months. I am brushing this under the rug, permanently Brian permanently."

"Are you sure you want to do that? I can't stop thinking about you, and no matter what I will always love you Tania Lane."

"Brian, one sex relapse session and you are feeling me all over again? Good God, you have women in and out of your bed. I am not in the mood for your rollercoaster ride again. There will always be some feelings between us, face it we have grown apart somewhat, I am getting married soon, to Derrick so deal with it."

"Think about it for the kids' sake, I really want this Tania, life isn't the same without you, I have managed to put a big band aide over the pain of losing you. But today that band aide came off and it's just pure love I am feeling."

"Band aide, first time I ever heard that line, Brian you are a classic. You dated that browning from the CVN Sports Cable Network for a year, and now that she left you, you suddenly want your family back."

"Sorry if being with her caused you pain, but just hear me out. You know how it is with these ladies; they only want athletes because of status. When she realized I wouldn't be able to financially be there she left, so many men in the sports circle been through her before me and not to mention after me. She was only a fluke, a no brainer, who I will be honest, gave me great heads, and yes I did like her until her money green colors began showing."

"Honestly Brian, I don't know what to think where you are concerned. If she was only a fluke then why flaunt her around in public the way you did? If she was only a fluke and you knew bloody well many men tossed her salad and jammed their steak knife into her beef, then why Brian Lane would you be with her? You disgust me at times; let's talk this weekend about the kids, right now I need to live with cheating on the man I plan to marry in two months."

I had to get him off the phone; I didn't know how to balance his words on a scale. I have been level headed for two years, not about to have him mess up my emotions with his need for comfort. I need to know if I too was feeling love, or just a sexual healing, damn it I now remember Brian discharged inside me, knowing my luck with Brian…Only God can prevent my eggs to not…Mr. Fertilizer.

"Mommy I want Spaghetti and meat balls." Yes you guessed it; BJ wanted my attention as usual. I had to take deep breaths, and tell myself this day will end in couple of hours, just forget about what happened with Brian and move on with Derrick.

Derrick gave me large sums of cash each week without fail, he wants me to start a business, he wants me to live in luxury and never needing basic things. He has principles, such as no kids until we get married, he wants so much for me, not saying Brian didn't just that Derrick looks at me in a manner as though I am a prize, a gem, a priceless treasure. Brian wanted to do for me, he basically preferred I stay home be beautiful with babies on my hips, knees, ankles, breast and on shoulder. Shoot if it was up to him I would have a dozen, and each would be playing Cricket.

Oh goodness getting up and walking around the apartment is such a challenge, Brian bruised my cherry, I am in total discomfort while walking. It feels as though it might take a week for me to feel better.

*** *

One week later, yes after my Brian Lane sex relapse I mustered the nerve to call Derrick and invited him over. We talked, kissed and made up like what lovers do, but I still couldn't shake Brian's touch in my mind just like that. Derrick wanted some loving, but I declined, made up some lame excuse and he bought it. Guess I am becoming just like Brian, a cheat and a liar, and as the saying goes 'If you live around bush, you will eventually become green.' Ok I made this one up, I think it's kind of unique and funny don't you think? Whatever the case is I was becoming a Star Girl, mimicking my Star Boy.

Then again Brian exploded his juices, and you know how fertilizing his juices are, so I am calculating another 3-4 weeks of excuses; because if my egg is fertilized how on earth will I explain to Derrick that a condom burst, when we both know that's a lie.

The entire week I wanted to share what happened with Jackie, but you know how that would have trickle down to mother dearest eardrum. I can just hear mother with her slight remarks like her famous, "What sweet you will sour you" I cannot stand these country bunking phrase, the other one she loves to say is "Every hoe have them stick of bush" and of course she feels Derrick and I are the ideal couple. Trust me she felt the same way about Brian, she was sweet on him, so sweet it was unbearable at times.

So I told Derrick what Brian and I discussed about BJ needs and what we thought would be best for him. Derrick and I have less than two months to finish planning a wedding, and within this time frame figure out BJ's living situation. Believe me I love Derrick, but I more fear my son's mental and emotional wellbeing, it not being that of normalcy. I know nothing in life is perfect but, scaring him is not in my deck of cards. Anyways let me at least front my enthusiasm about the wedding, look at it this way, it's like de javu. My first wedding I was pregnant with BJ, now the seconding time around I might be. Oh God help me, imagine you sent a good man and I might have mess things up thanks to sweet, sweet sex with Brian. Brian is not a curse, because you wouldn't have blessed him with such a large size tool, one thing for certain he knows how to give it to me proper.

Enough, enough, is bloody enough, damn you Brian Lane! You've managed to disturb my perfect world.

Tania
Showers of Blessings

Good morning sunshine, no more rainy weather, no more up and down life of infidelity with Brian. Today is the day of my wedding shower hosted by my darling sister Jackie! Yes I told her I wanted strippers, and lots of fun! Oh boy I am acting so childish; my pre-wedding emotions are riding on a high. I am so looking forward to tonight's event, and since my bridesmaids are wearing dark spring green dresses, I decided to wear the same color cocktail dress made exclusively for me by Heather Jones Designs from Trinidad. Her line is absolutely exquisite, I know you are asking why not a Jamaican designer? You see Derrick and I flew to Trinidad about 6 or 7 months ago, while there we attended one of her shows, it was fabulous! We stayed at the Hyatt Regency; our room was the Diplomat Suite overlooking the ocean.

I know after the divorce I called Brian and he was nasty to me on the phone, while with some fluke having the time of his life, probably pounding and poking her during his stay in Trinidad. For some women this might not sit well with them, to actually visit a place that had such memory. However there is so much to do in Trinidad, we chilled at a few beaches; Salibay was one of the most beautiful beaches in Trinidad. The day we went there a group from a church was conducting a spiritual function, they had nice drumming and signing. I believe they called it an Orishas Feast, singing and paying homage to waters collectively or mainly the ocean, sea, and river. The officiate was very young with dreads, he sang so well you felt the vibration so to speak. I believed they some of the followers called him Bishop D, or Baba Ham. Anyways that was neither here nor there for us, we truly enjoyed the singing, it was different and to some extent pulls your focus. The highlight for me was going to the Caroni Bird Sanctuary. Overall we had a grand and relaxing time. I hope Derrick takes me back for our honeymoon, according to him it will be a surprise. Guess I won't know until next week after I walk down the aisle as Mrs. Derrick Jones.

"OMG Jackie I am nervous and excited all in one!" I was speaking loudly on my cell while looking through the racks at Ariston Couture for a second dress just in case the strippers get me all too overly excited and wet in the wrong areas.

"Tell me something new Tania; you've been like this for weeks now. It's just a pity I am too tired to feel the same." Jackie sounded very overwhelmed on the other end. "I am happy for you sister dear, just exhausted from planning your big shower, plus mother wants me to do this and that. I never knew she was like you, into strippers and tons of other things that will remain a surprise."

"What you telling me Jacks, whose mother you talking about?" we both busted out laughing.

"Tania your mother, she isn't mine, she is very much so a hot mess. Blame it on cable television for exposing her to all sorts of kinky stuff."

"That's our mother you Jacks, remember she and daddy were busy rabbits? Is a wonder they never had 12 tribes of

Watsons. Anyhow my darling see you later Jacks, I need to focus on this sale rack…Love you sis."

What a wonderful day! So many dresses to choose from, I lost couple pounds so that my wedding dress will look perfect on me. Let me run into the dressing room and fit these three potential back up cocktail dresses. The first dress, was ok but kind of sort showing too much legs, second one was too old fashion and frumpy looking. The last dress an off white body fitted one shoulder with gold trimmings, now this was absolutely perfect! Even the sales girl went wild about the way it fit my curves and showed up my boobs. Seeing myself in this dress, scream seduction, girl on fire and God damn it I was ready to step into the new.

"Guess I will be taking this one." I told her, all happy like a kid in a candy store.

"Wow, wish I could buy myself one." Judith the assistant manager said while cashing me out at the register.

"Oh yeah, so what is stopping you? Don't you get 30% discount at the very least?" I asked.

"Yes, but I just found out this morning that I am 2 months pregnant, so my focus is on preparing for my third child."

"I understand, well after the baby there will be plenty more dresses to chose from." Damn Judith for sharing her pregnancy news, I completely forgot about me.

This conversation makes me remember my relapse with Brian, and yes I have put Derrick on a sex diet. This was kind of easy to do; I fabricated some stories about plans for the wedding, and not feeling well enough to have my body go through the motions. You name it, I said it, and he fell for it. I honestly put Brian's fertilizer juice injection out my thoughts; I have been under so much stress with this wedding, and the boys I lost track of my monthly cycle. This is not funny at all; shit man Brian knows how to get my head in a jungle all confused and emotionally off balance. Look Derrick is a serious cash cow, he has more money than Brian by far, Derrick family lineage owns a number of properties in Kingston, and not to mention in Montego Bay and St. Ann. His family comes from old money, construction and housing development is their line of business.

When I met him he pretended to be a worker at a site off Constant Spring Road, it took me six months to really know his position at D&D Construction. Derrick with all his money didn't have kids, yes and he was five years older than me. Here it is I might be pregnant with a third child, and it's not like I could pass it off as his, Brian features are very distinctive, there is no way a stranger could doubt my boys are not his. Father God, why did I open my legs and allow Brian to do what he did? I have to come up with a plan, I have talked tough about doing an abortion in the past, but truth is I cannot, I just cannot put my body through that.

***

My sister Jackie did a fabulous job with decorating this room for my shower. I remember her mentioning what Derrick said, he told her not to spare any expense, and at the end of the night he wanted me to feel like a celebrity, as if I lived in the States and I were Mariah or Celine. The room was in three colors to match that of the wedding theme next week. It was green, off white and gold, Jackie flew in a topnotch decorating team from New York, Focus on Divas Inc., they used elegant trimmings, and everything was uniformed. I felt like royalty, very special like a Queen about to marry her King. I am telling you the Waterfalls Hotel is the place to host your bridal events!

"Hi there Miss. Watson, my longtime sweets." A voice said from behind me.

"Oh my Jehovah! What a surprise for my special day! Look at Danny! Is that really you Danny?" I was so excited; you would think I am a fan meeting the sexy Tray Songs. Seeing my ace friend from school days was tons of fun.

"Yes honey all me. Look at you my sweets beaming and glowing like the way you should."

"Danny it's been a while I haven't heard from you, come here give me a kiss."

"On the cheeks or the lips" He asked playfully.

"Cheeks baby cheeks you know the lips are for hubby." I was so happy to see Danny; we lost contact for some time now. He sure looks fine, confident and poised. Pulling me to the side he whispered in my ears.

"I heard what happened with Brian, are you ok? You two were so much in love. I was shocked at Angela, not to mention this person name Dudley. These people put my sweets through hell, but I am here for you, we can play catch up tomorrow or so."

"Thanks Danny, we sure will talk soon." I see the gossip part of him hasn't changed, but it was nice to see him at the shower hope he will stay for the wedding.

There was a special chair for me to sit in, it was decorated differently from the others, and positioned where I could see the guests as they entered the room. What the hell! What is Marsha doing here?

"Hey happy bride to be, you look fabulous!" Desperate for friendship Marsha had to say something, I am not sure why she came. I totally disregarded her wedding invitation; I didn't even send a gift. But I guess she felt revealing the plots of her bestie was a shoe in for automatic forgiveness. Oh please, I will play along with a poker face. This was my day, my time to be me, and to be very happy.

"Thanks for coming Marsha, how is married life with Courtney?"

"We are good, we are very good, and actually we are two months pregnant!"

"Congratulations enjoy the sleepiness and being alone, because just now you will be popping them out one after the next." We both laughed, as she leaned forward to hug me. It's not that I hated Marsha, it just that she is a constant reminder of Angela.

"Oh I know you have moved on, but I wanted to share a bit of saga. Guess who got married, and now living a Rastafarian lifestyle?"

"I don't feel like guessing, just tell me." How transparent she could be, I had a feeling where she was going with this.

"Awww, well Angela, her life has completely changed. She is at peace with life, and the universe according to her. She even confided in me about the baby she lost after the fight with you.

"Marsha, don't you think you should move on from all this stale news, it's been couple years now…I really don't give two rats ass about anything Angela does, did, or didn't do." Besides to be frank, I don't see her as any wife material, more like desperate material. You know the kind that a foreman would buy either dirt cheap or extremely expensive in a crunching situation. But anyways good for her, as long as my construction man isn't looking in her direction I am all good.

"I think you should in this case Tania, that baby wasn't Brian's, it was Dudley's."

"Oh wow, such a surprise Marsha. Those two were in this plot together; this development doesn't come as a major turn political event or crisis. God knows best, that's perhaps the reason for him to take that baby away. Why bring an innocent seed that was made by two evil people?"

You see what I mean about Marsha, here I am having a great time and she comes here to remind me of Brian in a very negative way. She just got here not even one hour after mingling with the other guest. She drops this at again, my shower. Between her and Danny I don't know who the better of the two was. They were both great at sharing gossip, truth, mix-up and blenda blenda and whatever. Same difference with the acronym BPB, broadcasting people business! She only made my memories of guilt comes to surface, and actually piling on more guilt about divorcing him thinking the child was his. To be honest on the other hand, I am feeling sick of hearing about babies, pregnancy for the past couple of hours, rolling my eyes. Oh Lord again, and again I will say this, please don't let there be another Brian Lane baby in this very fertile oven! Brian Lane seems to have a dark cloud over my life, as though I was his baby machine. You know the saying, pop them one by one, galong boy. Let me get my thoughts clear, and enjoy this moment.

"Well that's her problem." Marsha has no sense of timing, why would she bring up Angela at my wedding shower. She could've sent me this information via text message or email, you know like 25 years from now.

I am living it up with a man who got it like that, and right now that's who I care about. I sound like a gold digger, but I don't care especially in these times where men are quick jukie-jam and not financially be there before or after the first night of humping. Don't judge me; just be happy I found me a real man who had cash! Anyways enough of the drama, the DJ Junior Culture is pumping some good music, I am about to go on the dance floor and show my mother some moves, and enjoy these sexy, tight muscle ass strippers.

Damn Jackie had stacks of $20 bills waiting for me. The first stripper went by the name of Mandingo, he had a six pack, and a ding dong that swing from left to right with ease and great rhythm. I told myself that had to be an extension for entertainment purposes. However Sledge Hammer was the highlight of the night, he prop me on his sculptured body, wrapping my legs around him. Let me not get into more details, because I was so tempted. Trust me with a mixture of Hennessey and Swedish Vodka I was high and highly on his front load that was covered by a tiny cow boy brief costume. As Alicia's song says *this girl is on fire*. Shoot my ass was teased, please and at ease. Ring the alarm send the fire trucks, someone needs to put out this fire.

Sleep, sleep, oh brother was I enjoying it until two little rascals climbed into my bed the morning after the shower. One was kissing my cheek and the other hitting me on the forehead to wake up.

"Morning Mommy wake up, wake up." BJ said politely as he peeled my eyelids causing me to slowly open my eyes, while his brother made baby noise trying to speak like BJ. These two were good at tag teaming, BJ lead and he followed.

"How did you two get in? Thought your Daddy was keeping you until tomorrow?" I asked as I kissed and hugged them both. My body was tired from last night, but as a mother when your kids need you; you just have to fine the energy from somewhere to be there for them.

"Morning Tania, I had to drop them off. The coach called late last night for an emergency training later this afternoon. I didn't feel like bothering Derrick to come pick them up." Brian carefully explained. Also I forgot I gave him a set of keys for emergency purpose. I barely looked him the eyes, been avoiding eye contact for weeks now. Brian only wanted to see me, he could have dropped the kids by Jackie or mother, but then again mother lives in Portmore. What am I saying, Jackie must be knocked out and not even know what day it is.

"Thanks Brian, I will take over from here."

"By the way I got my invitation to your wedding yesterday in the mail."

"Ok nice, see you then." I forgot to pull his invitation, oh snap what to do Dear Jesus. It might be very awkward for me. I will just play it cool, pretend he is not around, not sure why Derrick insisted he come, not sure if he was trying to be a stand up guy impressing my family or just wanted to rub Brian's noise in his wealth. Believe me when I say this, come next week not even Oprah's wedding can come close to mine.

"Mommy I want ice-cream and cake." BJ my little bossy hubby wanted me to get out of bed to feed him junk, glad it wasn't Burger King or McDonalds was his request, because I sure wasn't going to get out of bed for that.

"BJ it's too early for that, how about some cereal and fruits?" By this Brian left, the boys didn't even noticed. Hmm and I didn't even care what, how, or who he did, this emergency training was a bunch of baloney if you asked me. Anyways my two energy bunnies are here and I need to get my buns out of bed and cater to them.

Tania
Second Time Around

Two days before the wedding, things are so hectic between mother's annoying lectures about life, marriage, and growing old together with Derrick. Not to mention Jackie's whining, and my wedding planner Sharra from 3-D Planners who was experiencing last minute hiccups. My poor mind and body was a nervous wreck. I sent the boys to stay with Brian, I just had to. I know this was a huge wedding, but damn as the bride why do I have to feel so much pressure?

"Relax my darling, eat something, or let me cook your favorite stew peas." It was so sweet of Derrick to offer.

"I could use a foot rub instead, babes for some reason my appetite seemed to have disappeared during this madness."

Derrick gave me great massages; his hands are soft for a man in construction. His fingers are something else, shoot talk about moving from my toes to my calves, then above the knees to you know where. Once I said foot rub he knew I was gamed for some tingling, pleasure. Plus I wasn't wearing any underwear and that much he could tell from me walking pass him earlier. Derrick playfully slapped my butt, which made me a little wet. I really had him wrapped around me fingers, never in my wildest dreams I would have thought to find someone like him. Wait a minute; an idea just came to mind. How about we make love without a condom, this way if I am actually pregnant I can pass off the child as Derrick's. Sounds like a good plan; you can always leave it to a woman to concoct a devious paternity plan. Damn listen to me, I sound twisted like Angela and Dudley the two people who cause my first marriage to be in misery, and later ended up divorced.

"Sure, anything for my bride to be." Derrick was very calm, cool and collective, and just as I expected his fingers went up to my wet bush wick center. Do you get it? Bushwick Avenue Brooklyn New York, ha-ha a funny bone here, or I could have said Brian's Center Piece Center. Ok let me stop boring you with metaphors and enjoy my weed whacking moment with Derrick.

It has been weeks since he touched me, so you know I was tight, and as a treat for putting up with my lies; I gave him a nice clean delicious lollipop. I didn't follow through with my crazy plot, so he didn't give me his construction nuts and bolts screw driver work out. In the hospital the nurses use a phrase, finger stick, well in our case we only did finger suck. We both sucked, and he fingered.

"Oh, oh,...Derrick, take your time...shit baby that's it I am coming..." His mouth and head buried between my legs, man it was like he wanted to clean up the meat shop after a long days work. I am telling you Jamaican men are eating at female buffets like there is no tomorrow. They've become super freaks, some are into backdoor jamming as well. What's backdoor jamming? Shafting a woman's butt, as long as Derrick doesn't bring this type of jamming to our bedroom, all will be well. Front door, missionary, lizard lap, side borrows, back way, and occasional lollipop and we good to go.

"Derrick, please baby, leave some for later...oh that's it, that's the spot." Omg! He finally came up for air. "The boys are not here, we have the house to ourselves, let me enjoy myself, let me really have you the way I should!" And his head went back to the cherry spot; I kept my ass quiet and let him enjoy, the cookies, cherries, berries, whatever word to describe it.

'Sugar pie honey now, you know that I love you, I can't help myself I love you and nobody else.' My choice of music to set the mood one day before I walk down the aisle, I am in LOVE! Nothing and I repeat nothing is going to change this feeling! Dancing to the lyrics of various love songs, and packing my suitcase for The Courtleigh Hotel, where the wedding ceremony and reception will be held. I was beaming on a high!

Just a pity we couldn't book Jah Cure to sing in person at the reception. The DJ for the wedding was flown in from South Florida; his name is TC representing FlexxFm. Anyways TC will play a few exclusive songs from his not yet released album 'TC Master-Mix' as per my request. I got a chance to listen to some beautiful one drop love songs, I am telling Jamaican music is just the best thing since hot bread and butter with a tall glass of lemonade was discovered some 100 plus years ago. As for Jah Cure, to be honest we could decide on which of his song to officially dance to, it's a tossup between 'That Girl' and 'Only You'. Guess we should do both, and mesmerize the guests. Jah Cure songs are the absolutely best for weddings!

The boys are with Brian, he will bring them to the ceremony tomorrow, which is good, gives me time to focus on writing my vows and other final touches. I flew in a professional make-up artist from Just Because Hair Therapy Salon team, who will be at the hotel to do a make-up rehearsal; I have a final fitting at the hotel in couple hours as well. So Brian having the boys worked in my best interest.

After packing I called Jackie since it's my responsibility to pick her up in my wedding gift from Derrick. Yes, yes, a brand new red custom build 2012 Jaguar XF. Derrick is not just a great catch, but a wealthy well! A God sent one at that, well you know I had to blast my Jah Cure CD in my red hot car.

"How you so showoff little sis who cannot drive a Jag is a poor stepper?" Jackie said jokingly as I pulled up at her front gate.

"Who me? No sah, is my man you fi ask that question. Derrick loves spoiling me, and I just enjoy it sis."

"You too much, but anyways I am very happy for you. Let's hit the road, we have some many minor details to cover before tomorrow."

We got to the hotel in a timely manner, and we were pleased with the service so far by the clerk at the front desk. I was filled with energy, ready for the tasks ahead. Tasks, not an appropriate choice of word, perhaps my to-do list is better. Nonetheless I am happy, and in LOVE!

"Jackie please take a wild guess who will be coming to the wedding?"

"Who? My brain cannot play any trivia games right now."

"Old news, thing of the past Brian Lane"

"You are kidding me! I remember you mentioned his invitation to be pulled from the list, so how you managed to let this slip?"

"Honestly I really don't care if he comes, he has the boys and he will bring them, but Brian doesn't faze me like before. Derrick is fine with him being there, don't ask me why."

"Sure, right Tania, Brian Lane the love of your life in high school until two years ago no longer faze you…well I am 99 percent convinced my little sister. Just recognize you are getting older, and it's time you think about a solid and secure lifestyle for you and the boys. Plus the other kids you are about to have with Derrick. Although Derrick has money, he treats you like a Queen, and you two seem very much in love, so stand firm tomorrow as you commit to him."

"Oh Gees Louise, and Counsel General Matlock all wrapped up in one body; or aka Life Coach Jackie Watson! What a mouth full and then some, anyways you mean well, however I need a few minutes to myself there is a sudden need to call Brian. I haven't checked up on the boys since last night, it's already 4pm." I walked away from the front desk and sat in a sofa chair few feet from the bar, and dialed Brian's cell.

"Hello." I said, only to hear BJ.

"Mommy is that you? Where are you?"

"I am at the hotel BJ, and I will see you and your brother tomorrow."

"Daddy I am talking to mommy..." BJ was excited, and yet distracted as usual. Poor thing loves phone but cannot focus to have a long conversation, at his age what else can I expect.

"Hi Tania, how are things?" Brian asked.

"Busy, but finishing up a few details before tomorrow's event; how are the boys doing?"

"They are doing just fine, I hired a sitter to help me out she will be there tomorrow to give us a hand."

"Nice of you to think of using a sitter, listen up the tailor will deliver the boys suits by 7PM this evening so please look out for them."

"Ok no worries, I will text you when the delivery gets here, no need for me to call since you are very busy."

"Thanks Brian, give the boys a kiss for me and see you guys tomorrow."

Now that's taken care of from the list of things to do, next up, make-up rehearsal, then a little gathering with mother, Jackie and the bridesmaid. I feel so happy, and looking forward to having fun with the ladies tonight. But first Jackie and I are heading up to our rooms and unpack our suitcases.

"Tania, I am ready to go up or if you like we can have drinks before going to our rooms?"

"No, I need to at least see what my room looks like and layout my clothes for this evening. Besides we are going to have drinks with the ladies when they get here later."

"Make sense, oh yeah we have neighboring rooms, or connecting rooms so if you feel tempted to sneak Brian up I will hear all the groans."

"Funny Jackie, you are really being silly now, I could see if you said one of the Strippers from the shower. I am so over Brian, enough of him already."

"Oh I am just checking little sister, only checking your levels."

"Speaking of shower, hope Marsha won't be at the wedding! She pissed me off at the shower last week, with her Angela updates."

"I totally agree with you sis…Brian's invitation might have slipped through the cracks but Marsha was dealt with like national security."

"Yes ma'am, no drama queen around here." Jacks and I laughed but we were dead serious, Marsha was on our shit list for life if you asked me.

Now back to silly beans Jackie, she is my sister for life by default and that's one thing I cannot change, her silliness was getting on my last nerves though. Oh snap, just as I suspected, I was dancing too much while packing my suitcase and forgot to pack my green nail polish that I need in the morning for the spa session. I preferred to have my nails done hours before the ceremony, oppose to couple days before or even today.

"Jackie I have to run to the drug store, I will be right back." I yelled from my side of the room.

"Why Tania, what on earth do you need from there?"

"You wouldn't believe I forgot my nail polish, I will be back in a few though. You guys can start doing your make-up if the artist from Just Be…comes before I get back."

"Ok sis, get me some banana chips while you are at it."

"Yes greedy, what happen to your diet to help you squeeze your fat ass in your dress tomorrow?" We both laughed as I walked through the door.

We were on the 28th floor overlooking the city lights and sea that skirts downtown Kingston. These elevators work very fast, I was in the lobby within a flash. I stepped out and had the valet bring my car to the main entrance. Tipped him a $1000bill and then speed off. Oh I wished this was a convertible, I would let the top down and really relish in the rich status my car made me looked and felt. Yes, yes I am full of myself and so do the Cricket Wives, the Football Wives and the Rich Wives like me. Oh Lord I must confess, I am a gold digger a cocky one at that. Awww only kidding, I love me some Derrick Jones.

As I walked into the drug store you wouldn't guess who I saw? Guess, seriously take a wild guess. I saw three girl friends who are all pregnant wearing matching Lamaze Class T-Shirt. Now if I see another pregnant woman I swear I'm going to hit the roof with some cuss words. OMG, not me, not today it's like I walked into a store catered for pregnant women, this is hilarious or just plain out right spooky. Cho man I need this nail polish, few bags of chips for greedy bear, and then I am out.

"Excuse me miss." I tapped on the shoulders of a sales associate, she turned around.

"How can I help you?" And yes, she too was about 7-8-9 months looking to pop anytime now, who knows if she was carrying twins for her belly was like four watermelons. Life must be ruff for her to be so far along and on her feet working close to her due date.

"No, don't worry I see your condition I will look for what I need. Thanks."

"Are you sure?" She asked.
"Yes, I will find the bottle of nail polish; it shouldn't be too hard to locate in this store."

"Our nail polish is in aisle 12 to your right, far back section." Nola her name tag read was very customer friendly. I wished her luck, or God's blessings.

"Ok thanks, have a good day." Walking away from another pregnant chick, I wish this was a track and field that had room for me to run like Bolt.

So immediately before aisle 12 is 11, and there was a huge sale stand reading buy one get one free. Yes buy one pregnancy test get another free, so this way you make sure to test more than once in case you are in denial. I reached for the box, as it would appear in a figment of my imagination, my name was on it. *'Watson Pregnancy Test, Never Wrong and Always Right'.* All these signs for the past week, is simply telling me you are pregnant Tania Lane, wait Watson is my name. God damn it! Sometimes I get confused when I talk in my inner thoughts; you know when you talk to yourself internally, trying to rationalize life challenges. Taking a deep breath I reluctantly picked up two tests, and head for aisle 12.

"Will that be all?" The cashier asked as I searched in my pocket book for small bills.

"Yes that will be all." Now the challenge for me is, how do I urine on this stick and hide it from nosy Jackie? Remember we have connecting rooms, ding, ding, the light bulb went on. Tania when she is sleeping, it only takes a few minutes, but in the mean time I will hide them under the mattress. But what if I am pregnant? How do I pass this child off for being Derrick's? How? Bleach his or her skin and do some minor plastic surgery when the child reaches age 2 or 3; that's when their features begin to show, and the proof might be in the pudding.

Brian Lane and his nice juicy mushroom have my head hot now, plotting and scheming just like in the movies. Kill me dead my life will not become a soap opera, Angela and Dudley did it once, there is no way I am going to self inflict drama.

"I am back Jackie, did you miss me?" I yelled as soon as I opened the door.

"No, my little self-centered sister, did you bring my chips?"

"Of course greedy bear and I got my exact nail polish too."

"You are so obsess with that brand of Just Be…while you were out the make-up artist called. She is running late and her services come with a nail polish gift bag courtesy from the CEO."

"Well Jackie you know only celebrities gets special gifts from CEO?"

"And you are a celebrity, because of...? Someone needs to burst that bubble head of yours, come down to earth little sister." Suddenly we heard a knock on the door.

"Who is it?" Jackie asked

"Open the door it's your mother you two silly girls."

As Jackie walked to open the door I zipped my pocket book closed; inspector mother hen who is always fascinated with my bags was in the building. I just have to remain calm, cool and collective. Mother enters the room with an old sense of hierarchy, ranking head in the room and Jackie and I were to her lower aides.

"What have I missed?" she asked immediately.

"Nothing really mother, we are just here waiting for the make-up artist" Jackie answered. I kept my mouth shut, nervous hoping the make-up artist would knock on the door right this second.

"Tania, you look like a little girl up to no good?"

"Mother I can always leave it up to you...to spoil a good thing." I had to go on the defense immediately.

"Whatever in darkness will come to light Tania Watson, just wait and see." Again she had to come with her old, old sayings. Save by the knock or the bell whichever I was glad that there was someone at the door.

"Who is it?" Jackie the door keeper asked.

"Felicia your make-up artist sorry I am late." Felicia was God sent in more ways than one. She did an excellent job with our makeup rehearsal and gave pointers for everyday makeup use and skin care facts and myths. Dinner with my mother, Jackie, and the bridesmaid went well; I tried not to drink any Hennessy. Having a hangover the day of my wedding is a definite no, no. Plus I wasn't sure if I was pregnant, two glasses of red wine did it for me; besides I had to keep up appearances. If mother got a whiff I wasn't drinking any alcohol, her investigative brain will certainly start to work overtime in a jiffy.

The morning of the day I will say I do to Derrick Jones! I got up very early wasn't feeling myself. I had two pregnancy tests hidden from mother and Jackie who were both couple feet away from my room. You know what; I am worrying about nothing significant, I am not pregnant why bother taking this stupid test. As I was about to reach under the mattress for the test, my cell rang.

"Hello" I answered.

"Good morning Tania, how are you feeling?" it was Brian.

"Are the boys alright?" My first instincts were my boys since I didn't expect a call from him so early in the morning.

"They are fine, just I am not okay."

"What's wrong now Brian?" I felt a drag of nonsense was about to spew from him, in other words something lame rhyming with his last name.

"This might not be the perfect time to share this with you, however I have been feeling a number of emotional waves about you, it's hard to explain since this only happens when you are pregnant with our babies in the past. You see I was never able to express this being that each time you were pregnant we were at war with each other. Like the Israelis and Palestinians."

"Oh yeah really Brian Lane!" What did I say earlier, Brian and his obvious sabotage just cannot let go of me. "Brian honestly you need a shrink, and to find someone to jerk off this feeling, I cannot cater to you right now, and not ever, if it's not slightly related to our boys."

"Tania, please don't hang up, just listen."

"Okay Brian go ahead and speak."

"I will not attend your wedding."

"What? So how will the kids get here? How selfish and disappointing of you Brian?" I yelled on the top of my voice, he was irritating the hell out of me.

"There you go as usual, not letting me finish. I will have the babysitter accompany them for the entire day and drop them off at my house after the festivities."

"Brian I don't have time for you right now, you just make certain the boys are here you really don't have to come, it's not as though I truly wanted you to be at the wedding in the first place." I spoke my mind and hang up the bloody phone.

He can be annoying, and insensitive. What? One sex relapse has him all emotionally worked up. Come on Brian, we have been down this road over and over again for years now, after today I will need to set some boundaries, and stick to them. Why do men pretend? All along he acted as if I didn't mean that much to him, now he wants to plant a third seed both in my stomach and mindset. Brian has managed to upset my morning, on a day like today at that. You know what instead of throwing these tests in the garbage, to put my mind at ease and move on from him, I am going to do the test just for the heck of it.

"Tania, are you ok?"

"Yes Jackie, go back to bed, we have another hour before heading to spa. Go relax, I am fine."

"I am only checking since you were yelling on the phone with Brian sis. Well I am here if you need me."

"I am fine Jacks." I answered with reassurance from my side of the room without opening the connecting door.

Since she is already up, I needed to do this test real quick. Did I you tell how the bathroom at this 5 Star Hotel looked? OMG! If you remember watching Kimmora's reality tv show, the episode of her royal bathroom in her mansion out in New Jersey, well a version of that. You could wine and dine in this bathroom if you so choose. Yeah I am sharing this with you because I need a mental distraction myself. Tick, tock tick, how much longer *Dear Jesus?* Pacing the European marble tile, my nerves were in knots. Thanks to my high school sweet heart, aka my Star Boy Brian Lane. It was time for both of us to finally let go, but how could we, well me, if I am here doing this? Believe and trust that if this test result is negative in the next five minutes, there will never be another sex relapse! He could give the best whine, stick shift, or eat the pastry till I am dry, buckle my knees, damn Brian was really GOOD! Just the mere outline of his sexual skills makes me wet right now, hmm two more minutes and counting.

Alas, the time has come for the truth, why one month has passed since bloody Mary decided to not show up. Who the hell gave her a leave of absence? As I reached for the result, oh shit!

"Tania where are you?" Jackie was now in my room, not on her side where she belongs. Why this woman cannot take a hint that I need some privacy?

"I am taking a dunk Jackie." I quickly sat on the toilet holding the tube in my right palm has she sticks her head in the plush bathroom.

"Guess you just had to come in to smell my shit Jacks? I need some privacy; I will be out in a few."

"Tania you are absolutely disgusting right now!" She said before slamming the bathroom door and walked over to her side of the room. This connecting room business wasn't working in my interest at all.

One, two buckle my shoe, three, four shut the door, five, six pickup sticks, yes this pee pee stick with the result being…holding my breath…

"Tania Watson, you smelling your own shit inside here! Why are you being nasty to your sister? Come out that bathroom before I come in and drag your funky fresh ass out!" mother hen was in the room, coming to Jackie's defense.

"I need some privacy Mother, leave me alone nuh!" damn it, up till now I haven't seen the result. With inspector nosy in here it will not be possible after all.

"What you doing in there? Sitting around thinking about that two timer Brian Lane? Because I do not smell any shit coming from your buttocks." Mother barged in the bathroom standing literally two feet away from me, all up in my Kool-Aid, man if I had a bag of plantain chips this woman would be in it as well. Picture this, right, we were having a cowboy style showdown, however in our case there wasn't any guns, just eye contact, locked searching for weakness or in my case mother was searching for my lies.

"Okay yes I am here thinking about Brian, and no not in a romantic way for sure now mother dearest. He called upsetting me about the boys, and that he is trying to find a babysitter who is willing to work all day today and tomorrow. Are you satisfied now?"

"No Tania, you are holding more information. I noticed since yesterday; don't forget I made you, so no funny business around here."

"Mother please do me a favor and relax, just take a chill pill and go get ready for the spa in the next 20 minutes. Okay?"

"Tania, if you don't want Derrick, please let him go, do not humiliate this man! These are my final words for you today."

"Final words? I truly hope they are, mother I really hope they are." Shoot mother was my heart beat but also an annoying pulse.

She walked out finally, giving me the moment I needed to read this stick. The stick, this stick that will determine who will be the daddy if...

What the hell! After all this time the indicator screen had no line, had nothing. Wait I have to do this all over again. Let me check the expiration date, there must be a reason why the Pharmacy had it on sale.

Love is admitting when you are wrong, to make things right.
Love is not skin color, fat, and petite.
Love is defined by human emotions that are pure without hidden agenda.
Love is not setting sight on wealth, love is creating value.
Love is proudly showing the world your roots, no matter how your upbringing.
Love is not for sale, or does it have a discounted price.
Never mistake a person's ambition for a successful career to mean they will fall in love with you.
Love knows who you are, instead of trying to fit into a league that you will eventually have to sell your soul.
Love is remembering those who play a pivotal role in your life.

'Father in heaven, should I reveal the result of this second pee stick? For your judgment shall come and follow me for the days of my life. Your mercy I beg, as my love cup runs over, and over for Derrick instead of Brian. Let Brian stop following me, in my thoughts I pray. Let me know true love each day.' These are my words from inner to outer self as I stood in front of 6ft dressing mirror admiring my Heather Jones wedding gown. I've wrecked my nerves only to find the truth about my womb, my baby carriage, about the man I married, and the one I am about to marry.

"Tania you look beautiful!" Jackie said as she entered my side of the room. Even in my deep inner thoughts I am interrupted by her.

"Thanks Jacks, but give me a few minutes alone please I need to focus on my vows." Walking over to the mirror

Jackie hugs and kisses me whispering, "Today is your special day Tania, you will be alright, and he is *'the one'* after all these years he is *'the one'*."

The One

Pain is hurting from losing 'the one' from a broken heart.
A broken heart that only breaks once.
'the one' who will never ever forgive you after the pain.
'the one' who has shut the door and wishes you nothing but continued pain.
Will this pain ever end? Will I truly love again? Can I love again, is it possible?

Mirror, mirror on the wall here goes my vows after all. 'Derrick, crying tears became no more after meeting you. The day you asked for my hand in marriage, is the day I knew God sent you. I know we are like Adam and Eve, who was made from his ribs; we are one body, soul and one heart. You are the perfect man I ever known, the man I am happy to call my own.'- Well naturally I liked it, I wrote it today; this man Derrick Jones takes my breath away.

There was a soft knock at the door. "Who is it?" I asked.

"It's me Jackie, the ladies are positioned to walk down the aisle, and we are waiting for you to come down."

"You may come in sis, I am ready." I respond as I wiped the tears that flowed down my cheeks. Damn it my bloody make-up was running, this is an emotional day, the day I finally let go of my Star Boy Brian Christopher Lane and begin a new love chapter with Derrick Jones.

"Stop crying Tania, you are making a complete mess of your make-up. Come here let me refresh it before we head through those doors."

"Jacks, my loving sister I'm sorry for being mean to you. I needed time to reflect, as today is a very big step. Moving forward isn't easy, but I know today and for some time now that Derrick has completely won my heart."

"I've known too Tania, and I knew eventually after searching through your life's journey that beneath all Derrick's wealth and security that you would see his love for you, and your love for him."

"Jackie you are not helping with these tears sis, let's change the subject. Are the boys downstairs?"

"Yes your two spoiled children just arrived and dressed their part."

"Perfect! Let's go Jacks."

Wow the bridesmaids look so beautiful, my boys oh so handsome dressed in their off white suits with green bowties. The bridal party walked into the ballroom like a synchronized clock; to Celine Dion's hit song title 'Because You Love Me.' I chose this song after realizing how much Derrick loved her albums. Derrick was a mess; he played Celine's album on a few dates, and even tried singing a few lines. Believe me I gave him an E for effort, an A for the lyrics, and F for failing to have an impressive voice.

Holding back the tears as it was now my turn to walk towards the man I am about to marry, my new life partner. To my surprise Derrick chose my absolute favorite song, Celine's 'A New Day Has Come'. Taking deep breaths under this Vail, walking as slow as possible I saw my handsome husband to be waiting nervously with his unique sexy smile. Taking his hands into mine, standing in front of the Pastor, our guests sat quietly as the Pastor proceeds with an opening remark.

"Ladies and Gentlemen we are gathered here to witness the union of love, between a man and a woman becoming one under God's governance."

Looking at Derrick's frame, it was as though I was seeing Brian. I closed my eyes tight, opened them slowly and again it was Brian statue. Tuning out the words from the Pastor, squeezing his hands firmly into mine, I bowed my head, looking at my dress. It was the dress from my first wedding; I began to talk to the inner Tania. "Why are you showing me this? I am in present tense, Brian is in the past." I looked back down towards the aisle; just to be sure I was in the right frame of mind. Jackie did say that Brian didn't show up, am I losing my mind here?

"Derrick Jones you may say your vows to your beautiful and lovely lady." The Pastor instructed him.

"I Derrick Jones take Tania Watson to be my lawful wedded wife, to have and hold till death do us part. Committing my heart to yours Tania is my eternal vow this day forward, placing these rings on your finger to symbolize our perfect union and of course to let other men know you are mine." Our guests got a kick out of his last sentence; Derrick is a true romantic fellow.

"Tania Watson it's now your turn to commit your vows to Brian Lane." I could swear on 20 stacks of Bible these words came from the Pastors lips was I wearing a malfunctioned hearing aide? Again was I losing my mind?

Holding Derrick's hand, looking into his eyes, all I see is love. Closing mine to capture and store this look into my memory, I then opened it and saw Brian's face and not his. Tears' running down my cheeks, God why was this happening? I opened my mouth repeating the vows I memorized upstairs in my room, but there was no sound. Am I becoming deaf?

"Tania, relax and breathe." Jackie whispered in my right ear. Looking down at my dress, my dress from Brian and I wedding. Why wasn't I seeing the Heather Jones Collection I had on upstairs and walked down the aisle in few minutes ago? Why is he, yes him, Brian Christopher Lane inside me like this? Why?

"Tania, my love is everything okay?" Derrick realizing my distress whispered in my left ear, I sensed a level of panic in his touch now. Before he was holding my hands into his very firmly, now Derrick's palm was sweaty with a slight shake.

Shaking my head, wanting to open my mouth to say no, but for some reason my jaw was closed tight. Releasing his hands, I continued shaking my head saying no to his question, I cannot do this, lifting up my Vail looking into Derrick's eyes. Seeing the tears running down his face, he knew, he tried his best but it wasn't good enough.

The guests began loud whisperings; Derrick's mother's was as usual no holding bars. "I told you she was a waste of time." I heard a few more comments, but I blocked it out. Jackie began to panic as I stood frozen, unable to move my legs to run, to run from this embarrassing moment in time. Mother warned me, she was like a witch, or just a plain out right sensible woman. Was I that transparent all along?

"Tania, here is my cell. Go call him, go to him Tania just go." Hugging me tight, Jackie said these profound words that actually made my legs work. I began feeling them thaw out from that cold, feeling just few minutes ago.

Running like Bolt, at least it felt that way, my entire body wanted Brian, my heart was his. This baby is Brian's! Dialing his cell number, I can't believe I have it memorized; now pressing the send button.

"Hello Jackie, are the boys okay" Brian asked, thinking it was her on the other end.

"Brian, baby it's me, Tania. I need you now, where are you?"

"I've been sitting in the parking lot, outside the hotel waiting for you, listening to Brian McKnight's song 'Still'. Tania I still think about you, I am still madly in love with you."

The distance between the ballroom and the parking lot seemed like it would take forever for me to run into Brian's arm. Standing in the middle of the parking lot, so many cars parked thanks to what was supposed to be my wedding.

"Brian where are you, this lot is like a maze."
"Don't worry Tania, I see you, just know I love you and this time it will forever."

The End

REALITY BOOTH

I told myself no more reality booth, but after my interview with www.flexxfm.com on November 9th 2012; although it went well. A hour later I fell to pieces. Why? In life we must not take people or our relationships for granted. I fell to pieces because the pain of not finding his replacement is a serious struggle. Also remembering the good attributes he has, or what he shared with me then. Perhaps I am wrong to use him as a benchmark; however he is worth being such. I am not obsessed, what I am, is a woman living with regret for the things I have done to ruin a friendship not a sex-ship, a damn good friendship!

We often confuse great sex with love, he taught me the difference, he taught so many things and I wasn't paying attention. Now that I am doing so, my true message with this book series is to both men and women. That placing a materialistic value on your partner is not the right thing to do. Finding and cherishing the one who you are one with is absolutely priceless!

I am not saying to settle for a man or a woman who isn't ambitious in acquiring or achieving basic life needs.

Have I redeemed myself from writing this series? To answer honestly, NO. Living with guilt and trying to change is not an easy journey. But the good from this series is the reaction from readers, and discovering my passion as a young new writer on the block.

So to you sir, I am not obsessed, it's more about me appreciating the now in my life. Anyways thanks for reading and join me Spring 2013 for my next novel, 'Lady in Red'.

Made in the USA
Middletown, DE
30 December 2019